EL ESSENTIALS
— ON —
Developing Readers

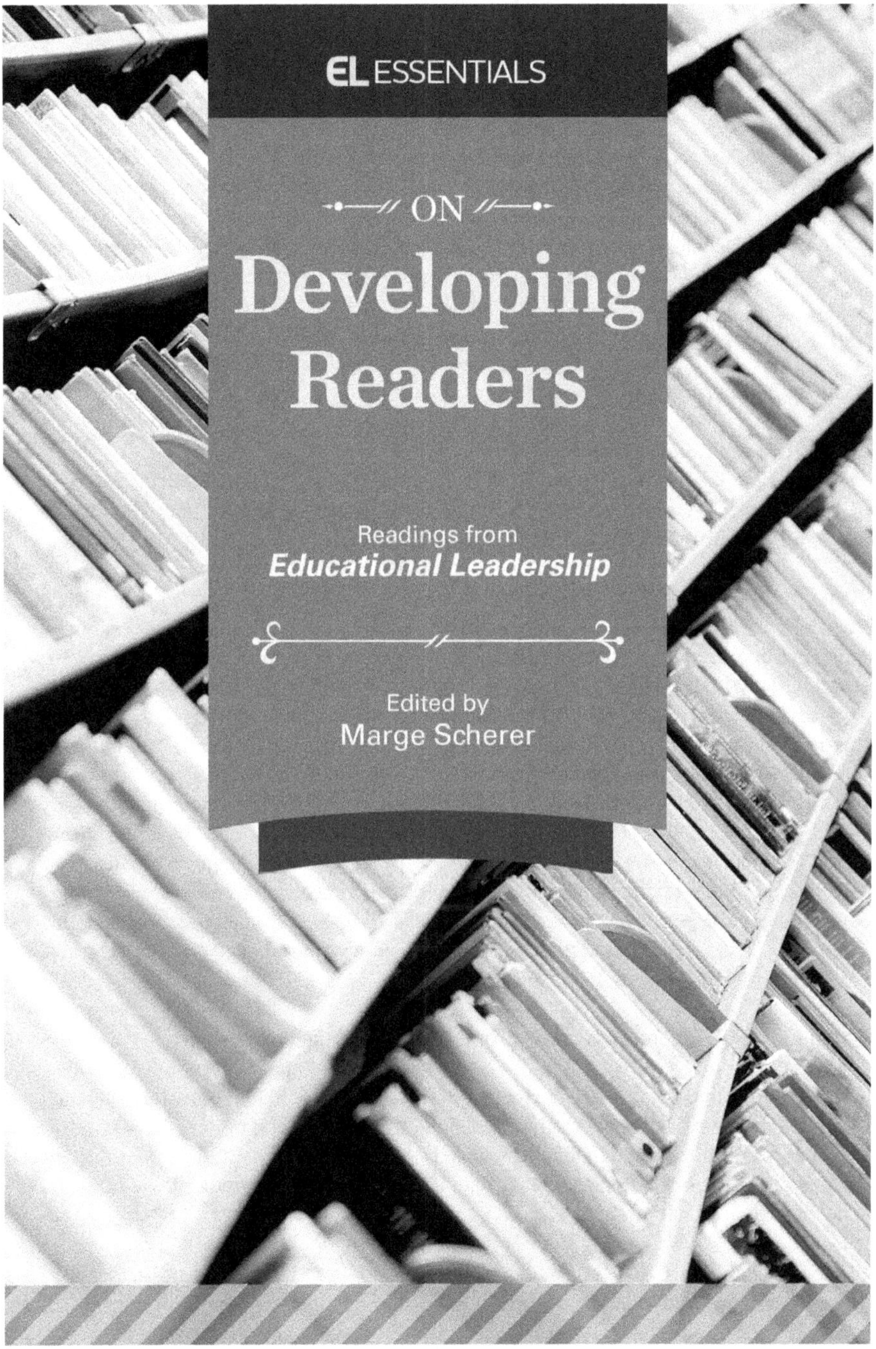

EL ESSENTIALS

ON

Developing Readers

Readings from
Educational Leadership

Edited by
Marge Scherer

ASCD
Alexandria, VA USA

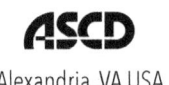

ASCD®

1703 N. Beauregard St. • Alexandria, VA 223111714 USA
Phone: 800-933-2723 or 703-578-9600 • Fax: 703-575-5400
Website: www.ascd.org • E-mail: member@ascd.org
Author guidelines: www.ascd.org/write

Deborah S. Delisle, *Executive Director*, Robert D. Clouse, *Managing Director, Digital Content & Publications*; Stefani Roth, *Publisher*; Genny Ostertag, *Director, Content Acquisitions*; Julie Houtz, *Director, Book Editing & Production*; Julie Huggins, *Editorial Assistant;* Thomas Lytle, *Senior Graphic Designer;* Mike Kalyan, *Manager, Production Services;* Keith Demmons, *Production Designer;* Andrea Wilson, *Senior Production Specialist*

Educational Leadership Staff
Margaret M. Scherer, *Editor in Chief*; Deborah Perkins-Gough, *Senior Editor*; Kim Greene, *Senior Associate Editor*; Naomi Thiers, *Associate Editor*; Lucy Robertson, *Associate Editor*; Judi Connelly, *Associate Art Director*

Copyright © 2016 ASCD. All rights reserved. It is illegal to reproduce copies of this work in print or electronic format (including reproductions displayed on a secure intranet or stored in a retrieval system or other electronic storage device from which copies can be made or displayed) without the prior written permission of the publisher. By purchasing only authorized electronic or print editions and not participating in or encouraging piracy of copyrighted materials, you support the rights of authors and publishers. Readers who wish to reproduce or republish excerpts of this work in print or electronic format may do so for a small fee by contacting the Copyright Clearance Center (CCC), 222 Rosewood Dr., Danvers, MA 01923, USA (phone: 978-750-8400; fax: 978-646-8600; web: www.copyright.com). To inquire about site licensing options or any other reuse, contact ASCD Permissions at www.ascd.org/permissions, or permissions@ascd.org, or 703-575-5749. For a list of vendors authorized to license ASCD e-books to institutions, see www.ascd.org/epubs. Send translation inquiries to translations@ascd.org.

All referenced trademarks are the property of their respective owners.

All web links in this book are correct as of the publication date below but may have become inactive or otherwise modified since that time. If you notice a deactivated or changed link, please e-mail books@ascd.org with the words "Link Update" in the subject line. In your message, please specify the web link, the book title, and the page number on which the link appears.

PDF E-BOOK ISBN: 978-1-4166-2227-7   ASCD product #116062E4   n3/16
See Books in Print for other formats.
Quantity discounts: 10–49, 10%; 50+, 15%; 1,000+, special discounts (e-mail programteam@ascd.org or call 800-933-2723, ext. 5773, or 703-575-5773). For desk copies, go to www.ascd.org/deskcopy.

23 22 21 20 19 18 17 16   1 2 3 4 5 6 7 8 9 10 11 12

EL ESSENTIALS ON

Developing Readers

Introduction: Calling All Readers by Marge Scherer 1

1. **Every Child, Every Day** by Richard L. Allington and Rachael E. Gabriel 3
   The six elements of effective reading instruction don't require much time or money—just our decision to put them in place.

2. **Starting Out: Practices for Use in K-3** by Nell K. Duke 14
   Learning to read and reading to learn are two sides of the same coin.

3. **Becoming an Engaged Reader** by Patrica L. Scharer, Gay Su Pinnell, Carol Lyons, and Irene Fountas 23
   We need to engage students right from the start in reading, reflecting on, and talking about interesting texts.

4. **Creating Fluent Readers** by Timothy Rasinski..........................34
   How to track and improve automatic reading.

5. **Reversing Readicide** by Kelly Gallagher 44
   Practices that boost the reading habit.

6. **Becoming a Classroom of Readers** by Donalyn Miller 55
   Teaching young readers what lifelong readers know.

7. **Unlocking the Secrets of Complex Text** by Mary Ehrenworth 65
   How to teach students to discover multiple meanings in the nonfiction they read.

8. **You Want Me to Read What?!** by Timothy Shanahan.....................77
   A sometimes tongue-in-cheek but always informative look at the questions surrounding the new emphasis on informational text.

9. **Closing in on Close Reading** by Nancy Boyles 89
   Three ways elementary school teachers can foster comprehension.

10. **The Challenge of Challenging Text** by Timothy Shanahan, Douglas Fisher, and Nancy Frey 100
    All about vocabulary, sentence structure, and other elements that make reading a complex act.

11. **Reading Through a Disciplinary Lens** by Connie Juel, Heather Hebard, Julie Park Haubner, and Meredith Moran 110
    Understanding how to think like a scientist, writer, and historian can provide students with new insights as they tackle text.

12. **The Power of Purposeful Reading** by Cris Tovani 121
    Why providing explicit directions about what students should look for in a text is helpful.

13. **Opening the Literature Window** by Carol Jago 129
    With help from the teacher, students can read books they wouldn't tackle on their own.

14. **Reading Moves: What Not to Do** by Richard L. Allington 136
    In almost every elementary classroom, you'll see students reading aloud and answering questions about what they read. It's time for that to change.

15. **Reading Disability and the Brain** by Sally E. Shaywitz and Bennett A. Shaywitz 146
    Neurological science combined with reading research provides the scientific knowledge we need to ensure that almost every child becomes a successful reader.

Study Guide by Naomi Thiers 157
   Ideas to try out individually or in a study group.

EL Takeaways: On Developing Readers 162

Introduction
Calling All Readers

"Hi, I'm Ishmael. At the beep, leave me a message about a book you love."

People who call Ishmael (774-325-0503) leave all sorts of messages about why a book has been important to them. On a day that I clicked on the website (*callmeishmael.com*), I found testimonials to the Harry Potter series, *The Little Prince*, *To Kill a Mockingbird*, and *The Sneetches* by Dr. Seuss. An especially interesting voicemail is transcribed each day so that readers can listen in to how *The Sneetches* changed the way a caller looked at race relations, or why another reader identified so much with a boy named Harry. Reading these messages made me smile at how the combined technology of anonymous phone calls, website trolling, and personal stories could together testify to the power of the book. It also made me think about all the books I still need to read—or reread and enjoy again.

Reading may be the most important and most complex skill students learn at school—the one skill that will open the door for them to all kinds of other learning. In addition, readers never know which book will change their life.

This collection of articles on the teaching of reading pulls together some of the best—and most clicked-on—articles on reading that *Educational Leadership* has published in the past few years. The articles cover what research says about the teaching of both reading and reading comprehension—from teaching phonics to improving fluency to tackling complex texts. *On Developing Readers* offers strategies for teaching informational texts as well as fiction. Most important, it also addresses how to inspire the love of reading.

In choosing these articles for you, the editors of *Educational Leadership* looked for the most practical and timeless pieces. Our purpose was to bring to your fingertips articles you may have missed the first time around or would enjoy rereading and sharing with fellow educators. This collection is especially designed for teachers striving to deepen their professional expertise, learning communities that are developing strategies to raise student achievement, coaches and principals looking for materials to share with teachers, and teacher educators who want to inspire teachers in training with ideas about the best in reading instruction.

If you like this book, you may also enjoy our collections on formative assessment, poverty and learning, and being a teacher. Let us know how you used these collections and which additional topics you might like.

Happy Reading!

—Marge Scherer
Editor in Chief, *Educational Leadership*

Every Child, Every Day

Richard L. Allington and Rachael E. Gabriel

The six elements of effective reading instruction don't require much time or money—just educators' decision to put them in place.

"Every child a reader" has been the goal of instruction, education research, and reform for at least three decades. We now know more than ever about how to accomplish this goal. Yet few students in the United States regularly receive the best reading instruction we know how to give.

Instead, despite good intentions, educators often make decisions about instruction that compromise or supplant the kind of experiences all children need to become engaged, successful readers. This is especially true for struggling readers, who are much less likely than their peers to participate in the kinds of high-quality instructional activities that would ensure that they learn to read.

Six Elements for Every Child

Here, we outline six elements of instruction that every child should experience every day. Each of these elements can be implemented in any district and any school, with any curriculum or set of materials, and without additional funds. All that's necessary is for adults to make the decision to do it.

1. Every child reads something he or she chooses.

The research base on student-selected reading is robust and conclusive: Students read more, understand more, and are more likely to continue reading when they have the opportunity to choose what they read. In a 2004 meta-analysis, Guthrie and Humenick found that the two most powerful instructional design factors for improving reading motivation and comprehension were (1) student access to many books and (2) personal choice of what to read.

We're not saying that students should never read teacher- or district-selected texts. But at some time every day, they should be able to choose what they read.

The experience of choosing in itself boosts motivation. In addition, offering choice makes it more likely that every reader will be matched to a text that he or she can read well. If students initially have trouble choosing texts that match their ability level and interest, teachers can provide limited choices to guide them toward successful reading experiences. By giving students these opportunities, we help them develop the ability to choose appropriate texts for themselves—a skill that dramatically increases the likelihood they will read outside school (Ivey & Broaddus, 2001, Reis et al., 2007).

Some teachers say they find it difficult to provide a wide selection of texts because of budget constraints. Strangely, there is always money available for workbooks, photocopying, and computers; yet many schools claim that they have no budget for large, multileveled classroom libraries. This is interesting because research has demonstrated that access to self-selected texts improves students' reading performance (Krashen, 2011), whereas no evidence indicates that workbooks, photocopies, or computer tutorial programs have ever done so (Cunningham & Stanovich, 1998; Dynarski, 2007).

There is, in fact, no way they ever could. When we consider that the typical 4th grade classroom has students reading anywhere from the 2nd to the 9th grade reading levels (and that later grades have an even wider range), the idea that one workbook or textbook could meet the needs of every reader is absurd (Hargis, 2006). So, too, is the idea that skills developed through isolated, worksheet-based skills practice and fill-in-the-blank vocabulary quizzes will transfer to real reading in the absence of any evidence that they ever have. If school principals eliminated the budget for workbooks and worksheets and instead spent the money on real books for classroom libraries, this decision could dramatically improve students' opportunities to become better readers.

2. Every child reads accurately.

Good readers read with accuracy almost all the time. The last 60 years of research on optimal text difficulty—a body of research that began with Betts (1949)—consistently demonstrates the importance of having students read texts they can read accurately and understand. In fact, research shows that reading at 98 percent or higher accuracy is essential for reading acceleration. Anything less slows the rate of improvement, and anything below 90 percent accuracy doesn't improve reading ability at all (Allington, 2012; Ehri, Dreyer, Flugman, & Gross, 2007).

Although the idea that students read better when they read more has been supported by studies for the last 70 years, policies that simply increase the amount of time allocated for students to read often find mixed results (National Reading Panel, 2000). The reason is simple: It's not just the time spent with a book in hand, but rather the intensity and volume of high-success reading, that determines a student's progress in learning to read (Allington, 2009; Kuhn et al., 2006).

When students read accurately, they solidify their word-recognition, decoding, and word-analysis skills. Perhaps more important, they are likely to understand what they read—and, as a result, to enjoy reading.

In contrast, struggling students who spend the same amount of time reading texts that they can't read accurately are at a disadvantage in several important ways. First, they read less text; it's slow going when you encounter many words you don't recognize instantly. Second, struggling readers are less likely to understand (and therefore enjoy) what they read. They are likely to become frustrated when reading these difficult texts and therefore to lose confidence in their word-attack, decoding, or word-recognition skills. Thus, a struggling reader and a successful reader who engage in the same 15-minute independent reading session do not necessarily receive equivalent practice, and they are likely to experience different outcomes.

Sadly, struggling readers typically encounter a steady diet of too-challenging texts throughout the school day as they make their way through classes that present grade-level material hour after hour. In essence, traditional instructional practices widen the gap between readers.

3. Every child reads something he or she understands.

Understanding what you've read is the goal of reading. But too often, struggling readers get interventions that focus on basic skills in isolation, rather than on reading connected text for meaning. This common misuse of intervention time often arises from a grave misinterpretation of what we know about reading difficulties.

The findings of neurological research are sometimes used to reinforce the notion that some students who struggle to learn to read are simply "wired differently" (Zambo, 2003) and thus require large amounts of isolated basic skills practice. In fact, this same research shows that remediation that emphasizes comprehension can change the structure of struggling students' brains. Keller and Just (2009) used imaging to examine the brains of struggling readers before and after they received 100 hours of remediation—including lots of reading and rereading of real texts. The white matter of the struggling readers was of lower structural quality than that of good readers before the intervention, but it improved following the intervention. And these changes in the structure of the brain's white matter consistently predicted increases in reading ability.

Numerous other studies (Aylward et al., 2003; Krafnick, Flowers, Napoliello, & Eden, 2011; Shaywitz et al., 2004) have supported Keller and Just's findings that comprehensive reading instruction is associated with changed activation patterns that mirror those of typical readers. These studies show that it doesn't take neurosurgery or banging away at basic skills to enable the brain to develop the ability to read: It takes lots of reading and rereading of text that students find engaging and comprehensible.

The findings from brain research align well with what we've learned from studies of reading interventions. Regardless of their focus, target population, or publisher, interventions that accelerate reading development routinely devote at least two-thirds of their time to reading and rereading rather than isolated or contrived skill practice (Allington, 2011). These findings have been consistent for the last 50 years—yet the typical reading intervention used in schools today has struggling readers spending the bulk of their time on tasks other than reading and rereading actual texts.

Studies of exemplary elementary teachers further support the finding that more authentic reading develops better readers (Allington, 2002; Taylor, Pearson, Peterson, & Rodriguez, 2003). In these large-scale national studies, researchers found that students in more-effective teachers' classrooms spent a larger percentage of reading instructional time actually reading; students in less-effective teachers' classrooms spent more time using worksheets, answering low-level, literal questions, or completing before-and-after reading activities. In addition, exemplary teachers were more likely to differentiate instruction so that all readers had books they could actually read accurately, fluently, and with understanding.

4. Every child writes about something personally meaningful.

In our observations in schools across several states, we rarely see students writing anything more than fill-in-the-blank or short-answer responses during their reading block. Those who do have the opportunity to compose something longer than a few sentences are either responding to a teacher-selected prompt or writing within a strict structural formula that turns even paragraphs and essays into fill-in-the-blank exercises.

As adults, we rarely if ever write to a prompt, and we almost never write about something we don't know about. Writing is called composition for a good reason: We actually compose (construct something unique) when we write. The opportunity to compose continuous text about something meaningful is not just something nice to have when there's free time after a test or at the end of the school year. Writing provides a different modality within which to practice the skills and strategies of reading for an authentic purpose.

When students write about something they care about, they use conventions of spelling and grammar because it matters to them that their ideas are communicated, not because they will lose points or see red ink if they don't (Cunningham & Cunningham, 2010). They have to think about what words will best convey their ideas to their readers. They have to encode these words using letter patterns others will recognize. They have to make sure they use punctuation in a way that will help their readers understand which words go together, where a thought starts and ends, and what emotion goes with it. They have to think about what they know about the structure of similar texts to set up their page and organize their ideas. This process is especially important for struggling readers because it produces a comprehensible text that the student can read, reread, and analyze.

5. Every child talks with peers about reading and writing.

Research has demonstrated that conversation with peers improves comprehension and engagement with texts in a variety of settings (Cazden, 1988). Such literary conversation does not focus on recalling or retelling what students read. Rather, it asks students to analyze, comment, and compare—in short, to think about what they've read. Fall, Webb, and Chudowsky (2000) found better outcomes when kids simply talked with a peer about what they read than when they spent the same amount of class time highlighting important information after reading.

Similarly, Nystrand (2006) reviewed the research on engaging students in literate conversations and noted that even small amounts of such conversation (10 minutes a day) improved standardized test scores, regardless of students' family background or reading level. Yet struggling readers were the least likely to discuss daily what they read with peers. This was often because they were doing extra basic-skills practice instead. In class discussions, struggling readers were more likely to be asked literal questions about what they had read, to prove they "got it," rather than to be engaged in a conversation about the text.

Time for students to talk about their reading and writing is perhaps one of the most underused, yet easy-to-implement, elements of instruction. It doesn't require any special materials, special training, or even large amounts of time. Yet it provides measurable benefits in comprehension, motivation, and even language competence. The task of switching between writing, speaking, reading, and listening helps students make connections between, and thus solidify, the skills they use in each. This makes peer conversation especially important for English language learners, another population that we rarely ask to talk about what they read.

6. Every child listens to a fluent adult read aloud.

Listening to an adult model fluent reading increases students' own fluency and comprehension skills (Trelease, 2001), as well as expanding their vocabulary, background knowledge, sense of story, awareness of genre and text structure, and comprehension of the texts read (Wu & Samuels, 2004).

Yet few teachers above 1st grade read aloud to their students every day (Jacobs, Morrison, & Swinyard, 2000). This high-impact, low-input strategy is another underused component of the kind of instruction that supports readers. We categorize it as low-input because, once again, it does not require special materials or training; it simply requires a decision to use class time more effectively. Rather than conducting whole-class reading of a single text that fits few readers, teachers should choose to spend a few minutes a day reading to their students.

Things That Really Matter

Most of the classroom instruction we have observed lacks these six research-based elements. Yet it's not difficult to find the time and resources to implement them. Here are a few suggestions.

First, eliminate almost all worksheets and workbooks. Use the money saved to purchase books for classroom libraries; use the time saved for self-selected reading, self-selected writing, literary conversations, and read-alouds.

Second, ban test-preparation activities and materials from the school day. Although sales of test preparation materials provide almost two-thirds of the profit that testing companies earn (Glovin & Evans, 2006), there are no studies demonstrating that engaging students in test prep ever improved their reading proficiency—or even their test performance (Guthrie, 2002). As with eliminating workbook completion, eliminating test preparation provides time and money to spend on the things that really matter in developing readers.

It's time for the elements of effective instruction described here to be offered more consistently to every child, in every school, every day. Remember, adults have the power to make these decisions; kids don't. Let's decide to give them the kind of instruction they need.

References

Allington, R. L. (2002). What I've learned about effective reading instruction from a decade of studying exemplary elementary classroom teachers. *Phi Delta Kappan, 83*(10), 740–747.

Allington, R. L. (2009). If they don't read much ... 30 years later. In E. H. Hiebert (Ed.), *Reading more, reading better* (pp. 30–54). New York: Guilford.

Allington, R. L. (2011). Research on reading/learning disability interventions. In S. J. Samuels & A. E. Farstrup (Eds.), *What research has to say about reading instruction* (4th ed., pp. 236–265). Newark, DE: International Reading Association.

Allington, R. L. (2012). *What really matters for struggling readers: Designing research-based programs* (3rd ed.). Boston: Allyn and Bacon.

Aylward, E. H., Richards, T. L., Berninger, V. W., Nagy, W. E., Field, K. M., Grimme, A. C., Richards, A. L., Thomson, J. B., & Cramer, S. C. (2003). Instructional treatment associated with changes in brain activation in children with dyslexia. *Neurology, 61*(2), E5–6.

Betts, E. A. (1949). Adjusting instruction to individual needs. In N. B. Henry (Ed.), *The forty-eighth yearbook of the National Society for the Study of Education: Part II, Reading in the elementary school* (pp. 266–283). Chicago: University of Chicago Press.

Cazden, C. B. (1988). *Classroom discourse: The language of teaching and learning.* Portsmouth, NH: Heinemann.

Cunningham, A. E., & Stanovich, K. E. (1998). The impact of print exposure on word recognition. In J. Metsala & L. Ehri (Eds.), *Word recognition in beginning literacy* (pp. 235–262). Mahwah, NJ: Erlbaum.

Cunningham, P. M., & Cunningham, J. W. (2010). *What really matters in writing: Research-based practices across the elementary curriculum.* Boston: Allyn and Bacon.

Dynarski, M. (2007). *Effectiveness of reading and mathematics software products: Findings from the first student cohort.* Washington, DC: Institute for Education Sciences, U.S. Department of Education. Retrieved from http://ies.ed.gov/ncee/pubs/20074005

Ehri, L. C., Dreyer, L. G., Flugman, B., & Gross, A. (2007). Reading Rescue: An effective tutoring intervention model for language minority students who are struggling readers in first grade. *American Educational Research Journal, 44*(2), 414–448.

Fall, R., Webb, N. M., & Chudowsky, N. (2000). Group discussion and large-scale language arts assessment: Effects on students' comprehension. *American Educational Research Journal, 37*(4), 911–941.

Glovin, D., & Evans, D. (2006, December). How test companies fail your kids. *Bloomberg Markets*, 127–138. Retrieved from http://timeoutfromtesting.org/bloomberg_education.pdf

Guthrie, J. T. (2002). Preparing students for high-stakes test taking in reading. In A. Farstrup & S. J. Samuels (Eds.), *What research has to say about reading instruction* (pp. 370–391). Newark, DE: International Reading Association.

Guthrie, J. T., & Humenick, N. M. (2004). Motivating students to read: Evidence for classroom practices that increase motivation and achievement. In P. McCardle & V. Chhabra (Eds.), *The voice of evidence in reading research* (pp. 329–354). Baltimore: Paul Brookes.

Hargis, C. (2006). Setting standards: An exercise in futility? *Phi Delta Kappan, 87*(5), 393–395.

Ivey, G., & Broaddus, K. (2001). Just plain reading: A survey of what makes students want to read in middle schools. *Reading Research Quarterly, 36,* 350–377.

Jacobs, J. S., Morrison, T. G., & Swinyard, W. R. (2000). Reading aloud to students: A national probability study of classroom reading practices of elementary school teachers. *Reading Psychology, 21*(3), 171–193.

Keller, T. A., & Just, M. A. (2009). Altering cortical activity: Remediation-induced changes in the white matter of poor readers. *Neuron, 64*(5), 624–631.

Krafnick, A. J., Flowers, D. L., Napoliello, E. M., & Eden, G. F. (2011). Gray matter volume changes following reading intervention in dyslexic children. *Neuroimage, 57*(3), 733–741.

Krashen, S. (2011). *Free voluntary reading.* Santa Barbara, CA: Libraries Unlimited.

Kuhn, M. R., Schwanenflugel, P., Morris, R. D., Morrow, L. M., Woo, D., Meisinger, B., et al. (2006). Teaching children to become fluent and automatic readers. *Journal of Literacy Research, 38*(4), 357–388.

National Reading Panel. (2000). *Teaching children to read: An evidence-based assessment of the scientific research literature on reading and its implications for reading instruction.* Rockville, MD: National Institutes of Child Health and Human Development. Retrieved from www.nationalreadingpanel.org/publications/summary.htm

Nystrand, M. (2006). Research on the role of classroom discourse as it affects reading comprehension. *Research in the Teaching of English, 40,* 392–412.

Reis, S. M., McCoach, D. B., Coyne, M. Schreiber, F. J., Eckert, R. D., & Gubbins, E. J. (2007). Using planned enrichment strategies with direct instruction to improve reading fluency, comprehension, and attitude toward reading: An evidence-based study. *Elementary School Journal, 108*(1), 3–24.

Shaywitz, B., Shaywitz, S., Blachman, B., Pugh, K., Fulbright, R. K., Skudlarski, P., et al. (2004). Development of left occipto-temporal systems for skilled reading in children after phonologically based intervention. *Biological Psychiatry, 55*(9), 926–933.

Taylor, B. M., Pearson, P. D., Peterson, D. S., & Rodriguez, M. C. (2003). Reading growth in high-poverty classrooms: The influence of teacher practices that encourage cognitive engagement in literacy learning. *Elementary School Journal, 104,* 3–28.

Trelease, J. (2001). *Read-aloud handbook* (5th ed.). New York: Viking-Penguin.

Wu, Y., & Samuels, S. J. (2004, May). *How the amount of time spent on independent reading affects reading achievement.* Paper presented at the annual convention of the International Reading Association, Reno, Nevada.

Zambo, D. (2003). The importance of providing scientific information to children with dyslexia. *Dyslexia* [online magazine]. Retrieved from Dyslexia Parents Resource at www.dyslexia-parent.com/mag47.html

---

Richard L. Allington (rallingt@utk.edu) is a professor at the University of Tennessee in Knoxville. **Rachael E. Gabriel** (rachael.gabriel@uconn.edu) is assistant professor at the University of Connecticut in Storrs.

Originally published in the March 2012 issue of *Educational Leadership*, 69(6): pp. 10–15.

Starting Out: Practices to Use in K–3

Nell K. Duke

Look for these seven features in primary classrooms that teach beginning reading and writing with an emphasis on informational text.

For decades, U.S. educators have believed that children first learn to read, and then, around 4th grade, they begin to read to learn. This belief has long been reflected in K–3 classrooms, where beginning reading materials have largely consisted of stories and where informational books have rarely been read aloud to young children.

The Common Core State Standards call for a major shift in this thinking. The standards expect children to be reading to learn as well as learning to read from the very beginning of schooling. Dozens of research studies suggest that young children can handle this shift (for example, Pappas, 1993; Reutzel, Smith, & Fawson, 2005). In fact, many children appear to be highly engaged by opportunities to read about the world around them and to demonstrate their expertise on topics through their writing (Guthrie, McRae, & Klauda, 2007).

Here are seven things we should expect to see in primary classrooms that are effectively using informational text to help students learn to read and write.

Informational Text Used from the Beginning

No longer should Dick, Jane, and Spot—or modern-day characters such as Mrs. Wishy-Washy or Fly Guy—provide the only grist for beginning reading instruction. About half of the time, materials should be informational texts. Although it's harder to find them, informational texts appropriate for beginning reading instruction are available.

Patterned-predictable texts, which are often used when children are still developing an understanding of basic print concepts and print-to-speech match, can be informational. For example, the book *What Grows Here?* by Santina Bruni (National Geographic Society, 2003) follows this pattern: "What grows here? Cactuses grow here. What grows here? Water lilies grow here," and so on.

Decodable texts, which can help address Common Core State Standards related to decoding, can also be informational. For example, the book *Who Has a Bill?* by Judy Nayer (Scholastic, 1997) notes the uses of different types of bird bills, as in "The bird will sip with it" … "The bird will tap with it" (pp. 2–3). The website TextProject.org has many sets of free, downloadable, four-page informational and other books written especially for beginning readers. (It also offers sets of free downloadable informational texts for older children to read over the summer months.)

In these examples, as in many informational texts for beginning readers, much of the information is conveyed through the photographs or illustrations. Through these graphics as well as the written text, children learn through reading while they are learning to read.

Informational Text Read-Alouds

Even with information-rich graphics, there are limits to the content knowledge that young children can comprehend through texts that are easy enough for them to read themselves. For this reason, approximately half of read-alouds should involve informational text.

Such read-alouds should be combined with engaging instructional activities—asking students questions about the text, having them discuss the text with partners and then share with the group, having them fill out graphic organizers as the teacher reads text aloud, and so on. Figure 2.1 gives some examples of how teachers can design such instruction to support students in working toward Common Core English language arts and literacy standards.

Sets of Related Texts

Gone are the days of reading a text on one topic, then another text on another unrelated topic, and so on. The Common Core standards explicitly call for reading sets of related texts: "Within a grade level, there should be an adequate number of titles on a single topic that would allow children to study that topic for a sustained period" (National Governors Association Center for Best Practices [NGA] & Council of Chief State School Officers [CCSSO], 2010, p. 33).

Text sets not only build students' knowledge, but also allow us to focus on specific Common Core State Standards, most notably Standard 9, which deals with multiple-text reading. For instance, Standard 9 asks that 1st grade children "identify basic similarities in and differences between two texts on the same topic (e.g., in illustrations, descriptions, or procedures)" (NGA & CCSSO, 2010, p. 13). Educators can compile sets of texts in advance on topics to use in read-alouds and small-group reading.

An Informational-Text-Rich Environment

Researchers and educators have long emphasized the importance of the classroom literacy environment for young children (for example, Wolfersberger, Reutzel, Sudweeks, & Fawson, 2004). Following this thinking, a K–3 classroom should immerse children in informational as well as literary texts. The classroom library should include large numbers of informational texts. Classroom walls should include lots of informational text: posters (museums and public agencies are a good

Figure 2.1: Using Informational Text Read-Alouds to Meet Common Core Standards

Grade Level	Sample Common Core Reading Standard for Informational Text	Possible Instructional Technique During Read-Aloud
Kindergarten	#2: With prompting and support, identify the main topic and retell key details of a text.	Ask open-ended, higher order questions: • What is this text mostly about? • What are the three most important things the author has told us? Have students use turn-and-talk to share their initial thinking, then discuss as a whole class.
1st Grade	#3: Describe the connection between two individuals, events, ideas, or pieces of information in a text.	Provide clipboards with graphic organizers, such as a Venn diagram or chronological order chart, for students to complete and discuss as they listen to the text read aloud.
2nd Grade	#7: Explain how specific images (e.g., a diagram showing how a machine works) contribute to and clarify a text.	Use sticky notes to cover an image in the text being read aloud. Read the written text and ask children what they can learn from it alone. Then uncover the image and ask students what more they can learn.
3rd Grade	#1: Ask and answer questions to demonstrate understanding of a text, referring explicitly to the text as the basis for the answers.	Establish a consistent follow-up question, such as, "How do you know?" to ask students after they initially respond to a question. Encourage students to ask that same question of you and of one another. Eventually, they are likely to automatically include how they know in their initial responses.

Editor's note: Standards referenced above are from National Governors Association Center for Best Practices & Council of Chief State School Officers. (2010). Common Core State Standards. Washington, DC: Authors. Retrieved from www.corestandards.org/ELA-Literacy.

source); informational articles in high-traffic spots (for example, where children line up); and children's own informational writing. Teachers can post directions—which the Common Core State Standards identify as among the genres that K–5 children should read—throughout the room.

For younger grades, dramatic play settings can include informational texts related to the theme, such as maps for a camping play theme. Older children can populate a "Did You Know?" bulletin board with interesting facts from texts they have read.

Technology in the classroom should also direct students' attention to informational text. Websites with informational text for young children, such as National Geographic's *Young Explorer!* magazine for grades K–1, should be bookmarked on the computers students use. A listening center should include recordings of informational books as well as literary texts.

A Lexically Curious Environment

Informational text for children typically includes a number of unfamiliar words. In kindergarten and 1st grade, the Common Core State Standards expect students to ask and answer questions about unknown words in informational text. Teachers should model and praise questions about words. So often in U.S. schools, children are praised for displaying what they do know; in this case, we want to praise children for revealing what they don't know—what they need to learn.

In grades 2–3, children are asked to "determine the meaning of words and phrases in a text relevant to a grade 2 [or 3] topic or subject area" (NGA & CCSSO, 2010, pp. 13–14). Even much older students have difficulty with this task, so explicit instruction is key. The teacher can use anchor charts to remind children of key questions to ask themselves as they make informed guesses about word meaning:

- Does the author explain what the word means?
- Does the rest of the page help?

- Do the graphics provide clues?
- Is there a glossary?

Coaching or guided practice is also important. In a lesson for 2nd graders, a teacher gave students excerpts from beloved author Jim Arnosky's book *All About Manatees* (Scholastic, 2008). The students' task was to use the context to try to figure out the meaning of specific words. For example, the teacher asked students to make informed guesses about the meaning of the underlined word in the following passage: "A manatee uses its highly flexible snout and upper lip to grasp vegetation to eat. Its diet consists of green aquatic plants." Notably, this vocabulary work had a larger purpose: Students were studying manatees and other endangered species to inform a writing project.

Teaching About Text

Even in kindergarten, you should see children talking about text itself—being metatextual. For example, the Common Core standards ask that kindergartners "with prompting and support, identify the reasons an author gives to support points in a text" (NGA & CCSSO, 2010, p. 13). Specific text features named in the standards for K–3 include:

> Kindergarten: front cover, back cover, title page, author, illustrator
> Grade 1: headings, tables of contents, glossaries, electronic menus, icons
> Grade 2: subheadings, captions, bold print, glossaries, indexes, electronic menus, icons, diagrams
> Grade 3: key words, sidebars, hyperlinks (pp. 13–14)

Across grade levels, the standards also refer to other components of text, including illustrations, topics, details, paragraphs, descriptions, procedures, individuals, events, ideas, and other pieces of information within a text.

Unfortunately, little research has been conducted on how to teach these text features to young children. In my experience, young children most thoroughly learn many of these features by producing the features themselves, either for their own texts or to add to published texts. For 2nd and 3rd graders, acquisition of text features may also be facilitated by engaging children with real-world texts for authentic purposes (Purcell-Gates, Duke, & Martineau, 2007).

Opportunities to Share Information Through Writing

One of the most important characteristics of Common Core–aligned K–3 classrooms is abundant opportunities for writing. This includes not only the narrative writing so common in primary classrooms, but also opinion or argument writing (30 percent of writing) and informative/explanatory writing (35 percent of writing). From kindergarten on, students are expected to participate in shared research and writing projects (independently in grade 3), recalling experiences and gathering information from sources. They are expected to use digital tools to produce, publish, and revise writing.

Clearly, the Common Core State Standards set ambitious goals for writing. Theory and research suggest that establishing compelling purposes and audiences for children's writing helps a great deal (Duke, Caughlan, Juzwik, & Martin, 2012). Although a story can arguably be of interest to any audience, informative/explanatory texts are written, outside schools at least, with a purpose in mind—to convey information to someone who doesn't already know that information and wants or needs to know it. In the classroom, we need to establish this kind of purpose for children's informational writing. And we need to pay careful attention to audience. A recent study of 2nd graders (Block, 2013) found that children wrote more effectively when they had an audience other than their teacher.

Some informational writing projects can involve children in writing about what they already know well. For example, 1st grade teachers

Sonali Deshpande, Mallory Kairys, and Wendy Rothman had their students write guides to 1st grade for kindergartners. The teachers used read-alouds and discussions to remind students of their own feelings and questions when they entered 1st grade. They shared examples of published guides to serve as mentor texts. They routinely reminded students of their purpose and audience for writing. On the day when the 1st graders delivered their guides to the kindergartners, the excitement was palpable. (To view samples of students' guides, go to www.ascd.org/el1113duke.)

Other writing projects can involve students in writing about topics for which they need to conduct research. For example, students might read texts about sea creatures and then write pamphlets about those creatures for the city aquarium. Or students might conduct interviews to learn about notable people, places, and events in the community, and then use this information to write articles for a class magazine to be distributed at city hall.

Regardless of topic, informational writing lessons and coaching should focus on specific attributes of writing called for in the Common Core State Standards—for example, the 2nd grade standards that require students to "introduce a topic, use facts and definitions to develop points, and provide a concluding statement or section" (NGA & CCSSO, 2010, p. 19). In addition, I recommend teaching students about other valued qualities of informational writing, such as grabbing and sustaining the reader's attention.

From the Past to the Future

The notion that children must learn to read before they can read to learn is a relic of the past. The Common Core State Standards hold high expectations for students around informational text, and research suggests that even young children can meet these expectations.

K–3 classrooms that implement the seven components described here, among others, not only give young children a jump-start on learning content knowledge but also engage them in reading and writing that establishes a firm foundation for their future literacy development.

References

Block, M. K. (2013). *The impact of identifying a specific purpose and external audience for writing on second graders' writing quality.* Unpublished doctoral dissertation, Michigan State University, East Lansing.

Duke, N. K., Caughlan, S., Juzwik, M. M., & Martin, N. M. (2012). *Reading and writing genre with purpose in K–8 classrooms.* Portsmouth, NH: Heinemann.

Guthrie, J. T., McRae, A., & Klauda, S. L. (2007). Contributions of Concept-Oriented Reading Instruction to knowledge about interventions for motivations in reading. *Educational Psychologist, 42,* 237–250.

National Governors Association Center for Best Practices & Council of Chief State School Officers. (2010). *Common core state standards for English language arts and literacy in history/social studies, science, and technical subjects.* Washington, DC: Authors. Retrieved from www.corestandards.org/assets/CCSSI_ELA%20Standards.pdf

Pappas, C. C. (1993). Is narrative "primary?" Some insights from kindergarteners' pretend readings of stories and information books. *Journal of Reading Behavior, 25,* 97–129.

Purcell-Gates, V., Duke, N. K., & Martineau, J. A. (2007). Learning to read and write genre-specific text: Roles of authentic experience and explicit teaching. *Reading Research Quarterly, 42,* 8–45.

Reutzel, D. R., Smith, J. A., & Fawson, P. C. (2005). An examination of two approaches for teaching reading comprehension strategies in the primary years using science information texts. *Early Childhood Research Quarterly, 20,* 276–305.

Wolfersberger, M. E., Reutzel, D. R., Sudweeks, R., & Fawson, P. C. (2004). Developing and validating the Classroom Literacy Environmental Profile (CLEP): A tool for examining the "print richness" of early childhood and elementary classrooms. *Journal of Literacy Research, 36,* 211–272.

Nell K. Duke (nkduke@umich.edu) is a professor of language, literacy, and culture and faculty associate in the combined program in education and psychology at the University of Michigan, Ann Arbor.

Originally published in the November 2013 issue of *Educational Leadership,* 71(3): pp. 40–44.

Becoming an Engaged Reader

Patricia L. Scharer, Gay Su Pinnell, Carol Lyons, and Irene Fountas

We need to engage students right from the start in reading, reflecting on, and talking about interesting texts.

We recently read a series of letters to the editor[1] in which one writer told of a 1st grader who brings home simplistic books to decode each night during tearful homework sessions. Another letter described teachers being "forced to use a scripted reading program against their professional judgment." Still another urged schools to "spend money on real books, not on basal readers and workbooks" and to stop spending "hours teaching phonics out of context, giving up developmentally appropriate activities in the process."

These comments raise the question: In pursuit of narrow, short-term goals, are we giving up something important?

Instructional mandates have monetary, social, personal, and emotional costs, and we must weigh those potential costs against the benefits. If we spend a great deal of time on whole-class drills that are too easy for some students and too hard for others, how will we meet the needs of all students? If we teach students through stories that do not make sense to them, what are they learning about the act of reading? If students get an overload of isolated phonics instruction, what will they miss in terms of opportunities to behave as real readers and writers?

This is not an anti-phonics article. We offer our credentials: As authors and educators, we have advocated for and written about phonics instruction for years (Dahl, Scharer, Lawson, & Grogan, 2001; Fountas & Pinnell, 1999; Pinnell & Fountas, 1998). Basic knowledge of the building blocks of words is essential. But we also argue for a higher goal. We want to make two promises to every child: We will teach you to read, and we will help you become a reader—a literate person who experiences the power and joy of comprehending.

These two promises are inseparable. Learning to comprehend is an ongoing process, a thinking process that expands across time as the individual encounters different texts, in different ways, for different purposes. Students do not first learn to decode and then become readers; they must be engaged in reading, thinking about, and discussing interesting texts from the beginning. Some important insights about readers, teachers, texts, and emotions can help foster this kind of learning.

Readers

Reading is thinking cued by written language. We cannot think for students; we cannot even directly show them the complex operations they need to put in place. But we can teach in a way that gives students an idea of what effective readers do and supports them in using these strategies daily (see Fountas & Pinnell, 2005):

- *Effective readers think within the text.* They pick up the basic information to understand what the text is about. Both fiction and nonfiction reading require literal comprehension. In fiction, readers need to identify the characters and follow the story. In nonfiction, readers need to understand the topic, learn facts related to it, and remember and know where to locate important information.

- *Effective readers think beyond the text.* They draw on their own knowledge and experience to make sense of what they are reading. They make connections to their own lives. They imagine what the characters are feeling; they infer what the author is implying. They make predictions and then confirm or disprove them.
- *Effective readers think about the text.* They step back from the text to notice how it is crafted, to appreciate its language, to admire the writing, or to critique. They notice the organization of the text and use it to find information; they recognize underlying structures that the writer has used to convey information, such as compare/contrast. This kind of thinking not only contributes to rich understanding but also helps readers become better writers.

Reading is indeed a complex thinking process from the beginning.

Teachers

For two decades, we have studied classrooms in which teachers teach for comprehension. In an effective reading program, teachers coordinate a range of instructional approaches: independent reading, in which teachers confer with individual students; writing workshop, in which students' experience with the writing process promotes their understanding of text; word study, in which students look at letter-sound relationships and word structure; content-area study, in which students build background knowledge and concepts; shared and performance reading, in which students must think about the meaning of a text in order to decide on the appropriate expression; and more.

Here we describe two highly productive teaching contexts: interactive read-aloud and guided reading.

Interactive Read-Aloud and Literature Discussion

You can think of reading aloud as providing students with a massive infusion of comprehensible written language. In every way but decoding the words, listeners process texts that they hear read aloud (Fountas & Pinnell, 2005).

Usually taking place in whole-group settings, interactive read-aloud is an efficient way for students to expand their vocabulary and concepts and share and understand texts. Through interactive read-aloud, teachers

- Create a community of readers.
- Teach students how to talk with one another about texts.
- Provide meaningful, enjoyable group experiences.
- Give students opportunities to process language and think about texts that are too difficult for most of them to read independently.
- Engage readers in thoughtful discussion.
- Model and provide group support for fluent, phrased reading.

Judy, a kindergarten teacher, had taught her students some routines surrounding interactive read-aloud. For example, she often paused and invited students to talk about their responses to the text, either in the whole group or in pairs. In the following example, which took place during a reading of *The Very Quiet Cricket,* by Eric Carle, notice how Judy helped students express theories about why a little cricket was silent. At this point in the story, the cricket had met several insects and each time had been unable to make a sound.

> *Teacher:* "The little cricket wanted to answer, so he rubbed his wings together. But nothing happened. Not a sound!"
> *Kyla:* What's wrong?
> *Teacher:* I'm wondering, too.
> *John:* Maybe he's just a baby and can't do it 'til he's grown.
> *Shada:* Maybe he can do it later with his dad.

Teacher: Maybe he's too little?
Mike: Maybe he lost his voice.
Kyla: My mom lost her voice once.
Cara: Maybe it has to be nighttime.
Teacher: Let's see what's going to happen.

Later in the reading, when night fell and the cricket was still silent, Judy reminded students of Cara's theory that the cricket could talk only at night. Students hypothesized that one of the other reasons must be correct or that it needed to get even darker. Later, when Judy read "and this time…" and paused for the ellipsis, one enthusiastic listener blurted out, "It made a sound!" The phrase "and this time," along with the pause, signaled to the listeners that the resolution was coming. The students in this kindergarten classroom were already learning how language works, how books work, and how to think while reading.

Interactive read-aloud sessions can become the foundation for small-group literature discussion. Guided by the teacher, a group of four to six students discuss a text together. Students in the group are at various levels of reading proficiency, but all enjoy talking about age-appropriate materials. Here is part of the discussion of a group of 2nd graders who had heard Vera Williams's *A Chair for My Mother* read aloud.

Charlie: I thought it was real scary when they were coming home and they saw their house burning.
Teacher: You thought that was a scary part of the story?
Janet: It's like in the book…we had a fire in our house and everything got black with smoke and it was scary, but we put it out.
Sarah: That's why they were saving so much money, because their stuff all burned.
Janet: But nobody got killed like happened on the TV last night. Nobody got killed in our fire either.
Andrew: They were putting money in the jar and then they had a fire.

> *Sarah*: No, they were just remembering how bad the fire was and how they didn't have any furniture and stuff.
> *Andrew*: Oh, they were saying why they wanted the chair?
> *Sarah*: Yes, but they still didn't have a chair and her Mama didn't have any place to sit.
> *Teacher*: I'm just thinking how they felt after all that, when they finally brought their chair home.
> *Fred*: They rode on it in the truck!

In literature discussions like this one, the teacher's participation is important, but students also respond to one another. Articulating thinking daily through this kind of discussion not only extends students' understanding but also sets a clear expectation that reading is about meaning.

Guided Reading

During guided reading, teachers support students as they read a challenging text that they could probably not read well without support. Guided reading is small-group instruction for students who exhibit similar reading behaviors and who read at similar levels. The teacher selects a text and introduces it; then each student reads the text either softly or silently. The teacher observes, notes students' reading behaviors, and sometimes interacts briefly with individuals. After the reading, students discuss the meaning of the story, and the teacher helps students practice processing strategies and engages the students in phonics/word study work. Guided reading may also include extending the text through writing, drawing, discussion, drama, or another kind of analysis (Fountas & Pinnell, 1996).

In the following discussion, Daniel, the teacher, introduces 2nd grade students to a new book.

> *Teacher*: Your new book is called *Henry and Mudge: The First Book*. It's very exciting because this is a chapter book. The

author is Cynthia Rylant. What do you think it might mean to say *The First Book?*

Janeen: Are there more books about them?

Teacher: That's right. This is the first book, but there are more books about Henry and Mudge, and you might like to read some of them later. [Daniel goes on to point out the characters and invite the students to talk a little about them, making connections to their own knowledge of pets. He also points out the table of contents and helps them notice that chapters are alternately titled *Henry* and *Mudge*.] So all through this book, you'll see chapters, and the title helps you think what the chapter will be about. You get to read the first three chapters today. You find out why Henry wants a dog, and you read about how he gets Mudge. Just look at page 11. On the left, you see Mudge.

Vera: He's a puppy. He's really little.

Teacher: Then on the right, you see some collars. Those are all the collars Mudge wore. What happened?

Vera: He grew really big!

Teacher: Listen while I read on page 11. "He grew out of seven collars in a row. And when he finally stopped growing... [Daniel turns the page] he weighed 180 pounds, he stood three feet tall, and he drooled."

Jorge: He's bigger than my dog.

Teacher: Yes, he's really big. Look back at page 11. Do you see the three little dots? That means that you pause and then keep going to the other page to finish the sentence. The author was helping us really notice how big Mudge got. OK, read the first three chapters, and if you have a little time when you finish, you can take out some paper and do a quick sketch of anything this story reminds you of.

In the interchange above, which took less than five minutes, Daniel provided information that would help students read with understanding. Notice that Daniel not only directed students' attention to details that they would need in order to read the text with literal understanding but also helped them notice the organization (thinking about the text) and connect the book to their own lives (thinking beyond the text).

Texts

Without interesting and engaging texts, reading instruction is joyless. We need texts that captivate students even at the beginning levels. At least three kinds of texts are important to provide a rich base for reading comprehension:

- *Books to read aloud.* Every classroom needs plenty of carefully selected, age-appropriate books to read aloud to students. There are wonderful picture books in every genre, including fantasy, informational text, biography, and poetry. You can read favorites again and again, enabling young students to internalize powerful language.
- *Leveled books.* Leveled books are categorized along a gradient of difficulty to help teachers organize their small-group instruction. They provide a ladder of support so that students can take on more difficult texts with teacher support and, in the process, expand their strategies for thinking within, beyond, and about texts (Pinnell & Fountas, 2001).
- *Classroom libraries.* Students should be able to choose from a rich variety of books that they can read independently. Students must experience massive quantities of comprehensible reading to build successful processing systems. Research has shown that the quantity of reading that students do really counts (see Anderson, Wilson, & Fielding, 1998). Students select books not primarily for their level but because the topic, the author, or the series interests them.

Emotions

One area is largely neglected in the current conversation about literacy instruction but is essential to creating successful readers: the role of emotion in memory and comprehension. Neuroscientists have proven that reading comprehension is a complex and individual constructive process. They have also found that beginning readers create networks in their brains to link what they see on the page to the language they speak. Emotions organize the neuronal networks required to think, retrieve previously learned information, understand, and remember (Ratey, 2001).

Parents and teachers know that there are individual differences in how children learn to read. Some children, when facing reading difficulty for the first time, quit immediately; other children enjoy the challenge of trying to figure out the problem and persist in their attempts. No matter how a child reacts to the learning situation, however, adults' responses affect the child's emotional, social, and cognitive development (Lyons, 2003a).

Michelle, a shy, withdrawn 1st grader, did not participate in classroom activities the first few weeks of school. When encouraged to react to a book read aloud, she became anxious and whispered, "I don't know." The concerned teacher called Michelle's mother to ask for advice. The mother said not to expect anything from "dumb Michelle." She complained that her daughter had had difficulty learning since she was born and would probably have to be held back.

If children repeatedly sense disapproval, they are likely to remember negative experiences and avoid putting themselves in those circumstances again. Michelle lacked the motivation and confidence to respond in class; she felt incapable of learning. Children who are experiencing difficulty learning to read commonly become frustrated. Continued emotional distress can create deficits in a child's intellectual abilities, crippling his or her capacity to learn (Levine, 2002). That is why we need to look for and support children's approximations or partially correct responses.

Consider the following example.

David had been classified as learning disabled in kindergarten and 1st grade by two teams of professionals (Lyons, 2003b). He was the lowest-achieving child in his 1st grade class, with little interest in classroom activities and a short attention span. He was unable to write any words and was reading below grade level. David was recommended for Reading Recovery, an individual tutoring program for 1st graders that builds on children's strengths. When David exited the Reading Recovery program 99 lessons later, he was reading at end-of-1st-grade level and was no longer labeled as LD, ADHD, or language delayed.

Carol, David's Reading Recovery teacher, noted that their relationship had contributed to his learning. Carol demonstrated a genuine interest in David and his learning, which helped change his attitude and increase his interest in reading. Carol also purposefully selected books and writing topics that built on David's strengths and interests, which further motivated him to engage as a reader and writer.

The brain's organization reflects its experience. If the child's experience is characterized by fear, anxiety, stress, and helplessness, then the chemical responses to these emotions become the most powerful architects of the brain (Damasio, 2003). Fortunately, emotionally positive learning experiences can change children's attitudes and provide motivation to learn.

A Higher Goal

Our challenge, then, is not only to ensure acquisition of basic skills but also to guarantee high levels of comprehension and a positive emotional response to reading. Educators have the resources and the knowledge to achieve this goal, but we will need to move beyond politics to do so. If we attend to readers, teaching, texts, and emotions and are willing to pursue complex solutions to this complex problem, all students can both learn to read and become readers.

Endnote

[1]Nancy Barth, Derek Boucher, and James Venable, in Backtalk, *Phi Delta Kappan*, May 2005, pp. 717–719.

References

Anderson, R. C., Wilson, P. T., & Fielding, L. C. (1998, Summer). Growth in reading and how children spend their time outside of school. *Reading Research Quarterly, 23,* 285–303.

Dahl, K., Scharer, P. L., Lawson, L., & Grogan, P. (2001). *Rethinking phonics: Making the best teaching decisions.* Portsmouth, NH: Heinemann.

Damasio, A. R. (2003). *Looking for Spinoza: Joy, sorrow, and the feeling brain.* New York: Putnam's Sons.

Fountas, I. C., & Pinnell, G. S. (1996). *Guided reading: Good first teaching for all children.* Portsmouth, NH: Heinemann.

Fountas, I. C., & Pinnell, G. S. (Eds.). (1999). *Voices on word matters: Learning about phonics and spelling in the literacy classroom.* Portsmouth, NH: Heinemann.

Fountas, I. C., & Pinnell, G. S. (2005). *Teaching for comprehending and fluency, K–8: Thinking, talking, and writing about reading.* Portsmouth, NH: Heinemann.

Levine, M. (2002). A mind at a time. New York: Simon & Schuster. Lyons, C. A. (2003a). The role of emotion in memory and comprehension. In G. S. Pinnell & P. L. Scharer (Eds.), *Teaching for comprehension in reading, grades K–2* (pp. 55–74). New York: Scholastic.

Lyons, C. A. (2003b). *Teaching struggling readers: How to use brain-based research to maximize students' learning.* Portsmouth, NH: Heinemann.

Pinnell, G. S., & Fountas, I. C. (1998). *Word matters: Teaching phonics and spelling in the reading/writing classroom.* Portsmouth, NH: Heinemann.

Pinnell, G. S., & Fountas, I. C. (2001). *Leveled books for readers.* Portsmouth, NH: Heinemann.

Ratey, J. (2001). *A user's guide to the brain.* New York: Pantheon Books.

Patricia L. Scharer (scharer.1@osu.edu) is Professor, **Gay Su Pinnell** is Professor Emeritus, and **Carol Lyons** is Professor Emeritus, The Ohio State University, Columbus, Ohio. **Irene Fountas** is Professor, Lesley University, Cambridge, Massachusetts. All the authors work extensively with Literacy Collaborative, a comprehensive professional development program for teachers of literacy.

Originally published in the October 2005 issue of *Educational Leadership, 63*(2): pp. 24–29.

Creating Fluent Readers

Timothy Rasinski

A growing body of evidence points to reading fluency as an important factor in student reading success.

Fifth grade has turned into a difficult year for Jonah. He is a bright student, but he has difficulty reading. Although he can accurately sound out the words he encounters, he plods along word-by-word, often hesitating at challenging vocabulary. His oral reading shows little attention to punctuation and phrasing, and it lacks expression and enthusiasm. Jonah can, however, understand material read to him. His difficulty seems to lie somewhere on the path from decoding to comprehension—in reading fluency.

Since the publication of the National Reading Panel report (2000) and other recent scholarly reviews of scientific research (Chard, Vaughn, & Tyler, 2002; Kuhn & Stahl, 2000; Rasinski & Hoffman, 2003), reading fluency has taken a front seat in discussions about student reading success and effective instruction in reading. Yet programs and materials addressing reading instruction and teacher training seldom tackle reading fluency (Rasinski & Zutell, 1996). This lack may be due to the fact that fluency has long been associated with oral reading, a form of reading traditionally viewed as having little importance in learning to read (Gibson & Levin, 1975; Smith, 2002).

Three Dimensions of Reading Fluency

Defining reading fluency may help clarify the issue. Successful reading requires readers to process the text (the surface level of reading) and comprehend the text (the deeper meaning). Reading fluency refers to the reader's ability to develop control over surface-level text processing so that he or she can focus on understanding the deeper levels of meaning embedded in the text.

Reading fluency has three important dimensions that build a bridge to comprehension. The first dimension is *accuracy in word decoding*. Readers must be able to sound out the words in a text with minimal errors. In terms of skills, this dimension refers to phonics and other strategies for decoding words. The second dimension is *automatic processing*. Readers need to expend as little mental effort as possible in the decoding aspect of reading so that they can use their finite cognitive resources for meaning making (LaBerge & Samuels, 1974). The third dimension is what linguists call *prosodic reading* (Schreiber, 1980, 1991; Schreiber & Read, 1980). The reader must parse the text into syntactically and semantically appropriate units. If readers read quickly and accurately but with no expression in their voices, if they place equal emphasis on every word and have no sense of phrasing, and if they ignore most punctuation, blowing through periods and other markers that indicate pauses, then it is unlikely that they will fully understand the text.

Assessing Reading Fluency

Teachers can easily assess each of the three dimensions of reading fluency. To determine proficiency in decoding connected text, calculate the percentage of words a reader can accurately decode on grade-level material. An accuracy level of 90–95 percent is usually considered adequate. Thus, a 3rd grader who is progressing normally in decoding accuracy should be able to read a 100-word text written at a 3rd grade level with no more than 10 uncorrected decoding errors. More than 10 uncorrected errors per 100 words indicates that decoding is a concern, one that requires additional instruction and practice.

Teachers can normally assess automaticity in decoding by looking at the student's reading rate. Reading rates increase as students mature, so the target reading rate increases as students move through school. An easy method for determining reading rate, and thus automaticity, involves having students orally read a grade-level passage for 60 seconds and then calculating the number of words read correctly (corrected errors count as words read correctly) (Deno, 1985). Compare students' scores with target rates (oral fluency norms) for each grade level (Rasinski, 2003). Readers who fall 20–30 percent below the target rate will normally require additional instruction.

The best way to assess prosodic reading is to listen to a student read a grade-level passage and to then judge the quality of the reading using a rubric that scores a student on the elements of expression and volume, phrasing, smoothness, and pace (see Figure 4.1). Students who score poorly may be considered at risk in this dimension of reading fluency.

By having students read one or two grade-level passages for one minute each, teachers can get a quick sense of their students' level of decoding accuracy, automaticity, and prosodic reading. Although such quick assessments may not be definitive, they do provide teachers and school administrators with a method for screening new students, tracking students' ongoing progress in the various dimensions of reading fluency, and identifying the students who may require additional assessment and instruction.

Figure 4.1: Multidimensional Fluency Scale

Use the following rubric (1–4) to rate reader fluency in the areas of expression and volume, phrasing, smoothness, and pace.

A. Expression and Volume
1. Reads words as if simply to get them out. Little sense of trying to make text sound like natural language. Tends to read in a quiet voice.
2. Begins to use voice to make text sound like natural language in some in areas of the text but not in others. Focus remains largely on pronouncing the words. Still reads in a quiet voice.
3. Makes text sound like natural language throughout the better part of the passage. Occasionally slips into expressionless reading. Voice volume is generally appropriate throughout the text.
4. Reads with good expression and enthusiasm throughout the text. Varies expression and volume to match his or her interpretation of the passage.

B. Phrasing
1. Reads in monotone with little sense of phrase boundaries; frequently reads word-by-word.
2. Frequently reads in two- and three-word phrases, giving the impression of choppy reading; improper stress and intonation fail to mark ends of sentences and clauses.
3. Reads with a mixture of run-ons, mid-sentence pauses for breath, and some choppiness; reasonable stress and intonation.
4. Generally reads with good phrasing, mostly in clause and sentence units, with adequate attention to expression.

C. Smoothness
1. Makes frequent extended pauses, hesitations, false starts, sound-outs, repetitions, and/or multiple attempts.
2. Experiences several "rough spots" in text where extended pauses or hesitations are more frequent and disruptive.
3. Occasionally breaks smooth rhythm because of difficulties with specific words and/or structures.
4. Generally reads smoothly with some breaks, but resolves word and structure difficulties quickly, usually through self-correction.

D. Pace
1. Reads slowly and laboriously.
2. Reads moderately slowly.
3. Reads with an uneven mixture of fast and slow pace.
4. Consistently reads at conversational pace; appropriate rate throughout reading.

Scores range 4–16. Generally, scores below 8 indicate that fluency may be a concern. Scores of 8 or above indicate that the students is making good progress in fluency.

Adapted from Zutell & Rasinski, 1991. Used with permission.

Teaching Reading Fluency

Instruction in reading fluency depends on the area in which students require the most help. Students with difficulties in accuracy require instruction in learning how to decode words. Although teachers are familiar with this kind of instruction, which develops skills in phonics and decoding, they may not be as familiar with methods for developing students' strength in automaticity and prosodic reading.

In my own instructional efforts to develop automaticity and prosodic reading, I use *assisted readings* and *repeated readings*, two methods that research has shown to improve reading fluency (Kuhn & Stahl, 2000; National Reading Panel, 2000; Rasinski & Hoffman, 2003). Students need to hear what fluent reading sounds like and how fluent readers interpret text with their voices.

Hearing fluent reading, however, is not the same as being a fluent reader. Fortunately, assisted readings can help. After reading a passage aloud to students, I ask them to follow along with me, first silently and then aloud, as a group. Sometimes I ask students to orally read a passage with a partner who is at the same reading level. At other times, I ask more fluent readers to read with students who are having difficulty with reading (Eldredge & Quinn, 1988; Topping, 1987a, 1987b, 1995) or I have students silently read while listening to a fluent rendering of the passage on tape (Carbo, 1978; Pluck, 1995). Such practices constitute a powerful strategy for improving fluency and comprehension.

Developing fluency in reading requires practice; this is where the method of repeated readings comes in (Samuels, 1979). Research indicates that repeated readings lead not only to improvement in reading the passage but also to improvement in decoding, reading rate, prosodic reading, and comprehension of passages that the reader has not previously seen (Dowhower, 1994; Koskinen & Blum, 1986; Kuhn & Stahl, 2000; National Reading Panel, 2000).

Passages meant to be read aloud as a performance—poetry, for example, or scripts, speeches, monologues, dialogues, jokes, and riddles—are perfect texts for developing fluency. I see many teachers converting their classrooms into poetry cafés and readers' theater festivals on Friday afternoons to give students the opportunity to perform the assigned texts that they have diligently practiced during the week.

The teacher plays a key role in developing prosodic reading skills by modeling prosodic reading in classroom read-aloud sessions and then discussing the specific oral interpretation that he or she chose. Coaching provides another opportunity for developing these skills by making students aware of their own interpretation of the text and moving readers toward deeper levels of interpretation and meaning.

Here are some comments I have heard teachers make while coaching students in oral interpretation.

- "You got all the words right, Thomas, but you read too fast. It was hard for me to follow what you were trying to tell me." "Eliza, the way you made each character sound different in this dialogue was fantastic. It was easy and fun to listen to these characters arguing."
- "I really like how you paused between sentences. This gave me a chance to think about the author's message. Now think about finding places to pause for just a second more inside longer sentences."
- "I loved how you made your voice strong and loud in this section. It really told me that this section of the passage was important."
- "Try slowing down here and making your voice a bit softer. Remember, you're trying to tell me about something mysterious. Tell the story with your voice as well as with the words."

As assisted and repeated reading, coupled with coaching, become part of the classroom routine, teachers can track changes in students' accuracy, reading rate, and prosodic reading. Jonah, our struggling 5th grade reader, originally read a 4th grade-level passage at 60 words correct per minute and a 5th grade-level passage at 52 words correct per minute. A 5th grader, however, should be reading approximately 100–125 words correct per minute during the first half of the school year. After just two months of working in small groups with a reading teacher for three 40-minute sessions each week, Jonah's reading rate on 5th grade-level passages increased to 84 words correct per minute. His accuracy, prosodic reading, and comprehension improved as well.

Several instructional routines for developing reading fluency show promise for improving reading in all readers. Fluency-Oriented Reading Instruction (Stahl & Heubach, in press) has students engage in modeled, repeated, and assisted reading of passages from basal readers. The Fluency Development Lesson (Rasinski, Padak, Linek, & Sturtevant, 1994) uses poetry, monologues, dialogues, speeches, and other performance texts to promote reading fluency. Fast Start (Rasinski, 1995; Stevenson, 2002) promotes early reading fluency through parental involvement.

Confusing Fast with Fluent

The new focus on reading fluency has great potential for improving the reading achievement of all students, particularly those who have not met with great success in reading. I am, however, concerned about how some schools define reading fluency and how some teachers teach it. In some schools, where improvement of the reading rate has become the chief goal of fluency instruction, teachers admonish students to "pick up the pace," regularly time them on their reading to encourage them to beat their previous scores, and engage students in daily reading exercises that emphasize speed over meaning.

This is a corruption of the concept of reading fluency. If we emphasize speed at the expense of prosodic and meaningful reading, we will end up with fast readers who understand little of what they have read. Fluency instruction leads to impressive gains when it provides regular opportunities for expressive reading through assisted and repeated readings coupled with coaching; it doesn't require explicit reference to reading for speed. Students' reading rates will improve as they become naturally more efficient and confident in their ability to decode words.

Fluency Into the Future

Research (Pinnell et al., 1995) suggests that reading fluency is a crucial factor among 4th grade students, but it can also be an important issue beyond the elementary grades. I recently worked with a group of colleagues from Kent State University to examine the fluency of high school students in an urban setting. We found that variations in the reading fluency of these students accounted for approximately 30 percent of the variance in their performance on Ohio's High School Graduation Test. Clearly, this finding suggests that fluency may be an issue that goes well into the high school years, especially among students from less advantaged backgrounds.

If teachers and school leaders are truly committed to leaving no child behind in reading, then they must actively pursue the goal of reading fluency in elementary and middle school classrooms. Existing scientific research on reading fluency indicates that it is an important factor in reading education and thus should be part of any comprehensive and effective reading curriculum.

References

Allington, R. L. (1983). Fluency: The neglected reading goal. *The Reading Teacher*, *36*, 556–561.

Carbo, M. (1978). Teaching reading with talking books. *The Reading Teacher*, *32*, 267–273.

Chard, D. J., Vaughn, S., & Tyler, B. (2002). A synthesis of research on effective interventions for building fluency with elementary students with learning disabilities. *Journal of Learning Disabilities*, *35*, 386–406.

Deno, S. L. (1985). Curriculum-based measurement: The emerging alternative. *Exceptional Children*, *52*, 219–232.

Dowhower, S. L. (1994). Repeated reading revisited: Research into practice. *Reading and Writing Quarterly*, *10*, 343–358.

Eldredge, J. L., & Quinn, W. (1988). Increasing reading performance of low-achieving second graders by using dyad reading groups. *Journal of Educational Research, 82,* 40–46.

Gibson, E. J., & Levin, H. (1975). *The psychology of reading.* Cambridge, MA: MIT Press.

Koskinen, P. S., & Blum, I. H. (1986). Paired repeated reading: A classroom strategy for developing fluent reading. *The Reading Teacher, 40,* 70–75.

Kuhn, M. R., & Stahl, S. A. (2000). *Fluency: A review of developmental and remedial practices* (CIERA Rep. No. 2-008). Ann Arbor, MI: Center for the Improvement of Early Reading Achievement.

LaBerge, D., & Samuels, S. A. (1974). Toward a theory of automatic information processing in reading. *Cognitive Psychology, 6,* 293–323.

National Reading Panel. (2000). *Teaching children to read: An evidence-based assessment of the scientific research literature on reading and its implications for reading instruction. Reports of the subgroups.* Washington, DC: National Institute of Child Health and Human Development.

Pinnell, G. S., Pikulski, J. J., Wixson, K. K., Campbell, J. R., Gough, P. B., & Beatty, A. S. (1995). *Listening to children read aloud.* Washington, DC: U.S. Department of Education, Office of Educational Research and Improvement.

Pluck, M. (1995). Rainbow Reading Programme: Using taped stories. *Reading Forum, 1,* 25–29.

Rasinski, T. V. (1995). Fast Start: A parental involvement reading program for primary grade students. In W. Linek & E. Sturtevant (Eds.), *Generations of literacy: 17th Yearbook of the College Reading Association* (pp. 301–312). Harrisonburg, VA: College Reading Association.

Rasinski, T. V. (2003). *The fluent reader.* New York: Scholastic.

Rasinski, T. V., & Hoffman, J. V. (2003). Oral reading in the school reading curriculum. *Reading Research Quarterly, 38,* 510–522.

Rasinski, T. V., Padak, N. D., Linek, W. L., & Sturtevant, E. (1994). Effects of fluency development on urban second-grade readers. *Journal of Educational Research, 87,* 158–165.

Rasinski, T. V., & Zutell, J. B. (1996). Is fluency yet a goal of the reading curriculum? In E. G. Sturtevant & W. M. Linek (Eds.), *Growing literacy: 18th Yearbook of the College Reading Association* (pp. 237–246). Harrisonburg, VA: College Reading Association.

Samuels, S. J. (1979). The method of repeated readings. *The Reading Teacher, 50*(5), 376–381.

Schreiber, P. A. (1980). On the acquisition of reading fluency. *Journal of Reading Behavior, 12,* 17–186.

Schreiber, P. A. (1991). Understanding prosody's role in reading acquisition. *Theory Into Practice, 30,* 158–164.

Schreiber, P. A., & Read, C. (1980). Children's use of phonetic cues in spelling, parsing, and—maybe—reading. *Bulletin of the Orton Society, 30,* 209–224.

Smith, N. B. (2002). *American reading instruction* (Special ed.). Newark, DE: International Reading Association.

Stahl, S., & Heubach, K. (2005). Fluency-oriented reading instruction. *Elementary School Journal.*

Stevenson, B. (2002). *Efficacy of the Fast Start parent tutoring program in the development of reading skills of first grade students.* Unpublished doctoral dissertation, The Ohio State University, Columbus.

Topping, K. (1987a). Paired reading: A powerful technique for parent use. *The Reading Teacher, 40,* 604–614.

Topping, K. (1987b). Peer tutored paired reading: Outcome data from ten projects. *Educational Psychology, 7,* 133–145.

Topping, K. (1995). *Paired reading, spelling, and writing.* New York: Cassell.

Zutell, J., & Rasinski, T. V. (1991). Training teachers to attend to their students' oral reading fluency. *Theory Into Practice, 30,* 211–217.

Timothy Rasinski (trasinsk@kent.edu) is Professor in the Department of Teaching Leadership and Curriculum Studies at Kent State University.

Originally published in the March 2004 issue of *Educational Leadership, 61*(6): pp. 46–51.

Reversing Readicide

Kelly Gallagher

Schools have become unwitting coconspirators in the decline of reading.

On a recent cross-country flight, I found myself sitting next to the president of a multimillion dollar computer software company. To keep his business competitive, he told me, his organization regularly recruits employees from top universities. When I asked him how his current recruitment efforts were going, he said that over the past few years it had become increasingly challenging to find qualified workers. It isn't difficult finding smart candidates; the problem is finding smart people who can think.

This conversation often comes to mind as I teach my students at Magnolia High School in Anaheim, California. My current freshmen entered 2nd grade as No Child Left Behind (NCLB) became law. Almost their entire school experience has been shaped by test preparation. These students have already spent years in schools where teachers and administrators have confused covering massive amounts of material with teaching students how to think and read critically.

One major drawback of having students spend their formative years memorizing facts is that facts change. Robert J. Sternberg, former president of the American Psychological Association, notes that the "facts" he learned years ago in his introductory psychology course matter little today. Instead of pounding facts into students' heads, Sternberg (2007/2008) suggests, schools should nurture attributes and skills that are foundational to becoming expert citizens, such as solving problems creatively, working well in teams, and knowing how to lose as well as win.

I fear that in the rush to prepare students for the next round of exams, schools are neglecting attributes like these. And if we are to guide students to become thoughtful adults who possess such qualities, we must face the elephant in the room: U.S. students' lack of reading proficiency and their general disinclination to read.

The signs are not encouraging. Consider the following points taken from a 2006 report on adolescent literacy by the National Council of Teachers of English:

- The 2004 National Assessment of Educational Progress showed that U.S. secondary school students are reading at a rate significantly below expected levels.
- The Alliance for Excellent Education points out that 8.7 million secondary students—one in four—are unable to read and comprehend the material in their textbooks.
- The 2005 ACT College Readiness Benchmark for Reading found that only one-half of the students tested were ready for college-level reading. Reading scores were the lowest in a decade.

Young people in the United States are not just substandard readers, they are increasingly reluctant readers—even in their free time. In the National Endowment for the Arts' comprehensive 2007 survey of American reading, *To Read or Not to Read*, researchers found that a "calamitous, universal falling off of reading" occurs for many students at around age 13 and often continues through the rest of these students' lives.

Educators know the commonly cited culprits behind the decline of reading: poverty, lack of parent education, print-poor environments at home, second-language issues, the overscheduling of children, and competition from electronic media. To this list, I would like to add a factor I call *readicide*, meaning practices educators employ to raise reading scores that actually kill students' love of reading. Readicide is occurring, ironically, in the one place where a love of reading should be fostered—schools.

How have schools become coconspirators in the decline of reading? I suggest four contributing factors: (1) Schools act as though they value the development of test takers more than the development of readers, (2) Schools are limiting authentic reading experiences, (3) Teachers are overteaching books, and (4) Teachers are undereaching books. Let's look at how each of these practices leads to readicide, and examine steps teachers can take to counteract them.

Factor 1: Schools develop test takers instead of readers.

A curriculum steeped in test preparation drives shallow teaching and learning. Consider, for example, the monumental task confronting social science teachers in California, who must teach the following standard from the 10th grade curriculum:

Compare and contrast the Glorious Revolution of England, the American Revolution, and the French Revolution and their enduring effects worldwide on the political expectations for self-government and individual liberty.

How long would it take to teach this standard so that students acquire in-depth understanding? A teacher could easily spend an entire year on this single standard—but this is only one of 49 similar standards 10th grade teachers must cover.

I purposefully use the word *cover* because that is what teachers must do to get students through the amount of material required to generate test scores that will appease administrators, school board members, and parents. Breadth is now winning out over depth in most subjects. Science curriculum frameworks in the United States, for example, are loaded with more topics than frameworks of other countries (Cavanagh, 2009).

It's good to have standards for what students should know, of course. But when there are too many standards, in-depth teaching gets thrown out the window, and schools start producing memorizers instead of thinkers. And when coverage trumps depth, close reading— the kind students need to develop their ability to read critically— gives way to surface-level, "one and done" reading.

Reversing the Trend

We must ask whether teaching in a coverage mode serves the long-term interests of our students as readers. If we look at students' critical reading scores on the Scholastic Aptitude Test (SAT) from 2002 to 2009, during the time NCLB has been in effect, we see a slight increase in points for several years, followed by a decline to below the average score for 2002 (Gewertz, 2009). Isn't it interesting that although many districts tout rising test scores at the local level, reading scores on a key national assessment are in decline?

One recent study, in fact, found that nearly one-third of states have lowered their academic proficiency standards in reading and mathematics to make it easier for schools to make adequate yearly progress under NCLB (Dillon, 2009). Reading scores may be "rising" in districts across the country, but when one looks at a national assessment like the SAT, it seems our brightest students are actually regressing.

Clearly, the "coverage" approach is not working. It's time to bring depth back into the curriculum. Our students would be much better served if we taught them fewer concepts, slowed down, and taught them to think.

Factor 2: Schools limit authentic reading experiences.

I currently teach five periods of 9th grade English at Magnolia High School in Anaheim, California. More than one-half of my students are socio-economically disadvantaged. The student body is 68 percent Hispanic; more than one-third are English language learners, and nearly 40 languages are spoken on campus.

Although my students have passed innumerable tests in their journey to high school, they are shockingly unaware of what is happening in the world. For example, only a small percentage can tell me the name of the vice president of the United States. Not a single student can name the chief justice of the Supreme Court, and only a handful can define the rights protected by the 4th amendment to the U.S. Constitution. On the other hand, almost every student can name the four judges on *American Idol*. More than half of my seniors last year did not understand that newspapers have editorial sections. These students have since passed all their tests and graduated; they are the next generation in charge.

I point this out not to bash my students, many of whom are exceptionally bright. My concern is simpler: Schools are not doing the job they once did of engaging students in the kinds of reading that enable them to become literate, well-informed adults. Instead, as students progress through our schools, they are forced to read more and more worksheets focused on isolated facts.

Reversing the Trend

Teachers should be guiding students in real-world reading, assigning critical reading of magazines, newspapers, Web sites, and blogs that provide background knowledge about U.S. society, key political players and issues, and students' own role as informed participants. At Magnolia High, for example, all students are given an article of the week to read every Monday. These articles are selected to shore up students' lack of prior knowledge about life outside high school.

Factor 3: Teachers overteach books.

On my desk is a copy of the Los Angeles Unified School District's guide to teaching *To Kill a Mockingbird*. This guide contains overarching questions, chapter study questions, essay questions, vocabulary lessons, activities for specific chapters, guided reading lessons, directions for setting up a writer's notebook, literary analysis questions, collaborative activities, handouts, transparencies, 20 detailed lessons, quizzes, and projects. The guide is 122 pages long and includes numerous pages listing goals and "habits of thinking" that teachers should foster in students.

Why is this guide so exhaustive? Because it's aligned to the massive number of standards found on California's standardized exams each spring. As a result, teachers are driven into a "teach all things in all books" approach.

I am not suggesting that the goals in this unit of study are not worthy; they are. But using *all* these lessons to teach one novel, which teachers must do if they are to prepare their students for standardized exams, is a recipe for readicide. If I were to follow this curriculum guide step-by-step in my own classroom, there is little doubt my students would exit my class hating *To Kill a Mockingbird*—and possibly all reading—forever.

In the quest to prepare students for every standard that might be covered on this year's exams, teachers now chop great books into so many pieces that the books cease to be great. One teacher I observed, for example, required students to share their thinking on a sticky note on every page of *Romeo and Juliet*. As a result, this timeless work became an extended worksheet. Its beauty—its value—got lost in a sea of sticky notes. Imagine going to see a great movie, only to have the projectionist stop the film every four minutes to see if you are taking notes. Now imagine being forced to read a novel this way, and you'll see how overteaching destroys students' desire to read.

The antidote to this practice is not to simply assign great books and turn students loose—this practice leads to its own dangers—but to find what I call the *sweet spot* of instruction that gives students just the right amount of support for complex texts. Let's look at the flip side of how many schools introduce students to literature.

Factor 4: Teachers underteach books.

This may seem strange coming on the heels of my argument that too much teaching can kill a book, but underteaching a book can have equally devastating consequences.

At the end of her 10th grade year, my daughter was handed *The Grapes of Wrath* and told to read it over the summer. Her teacher did not "frame" the novel for her in any way; she provided little, if any, background information or support, and she communicated no purpose for reading the book other than to prepare for an exam on the first day of school. The assumption was that, as an honor student, my daughter could handle the task. You might guess what happened. My daughter started to read the novel, became frustrated, turned to a summary on Spark Notes, passed the test, and grew into an adult who still thinks *The Grapes of Wrath* is a lousy book.

If students could read academic texts or challenging literary works by themselves, they would not need teachers. But, of course, most cannot gain the full benefit from—and enjoy—difficult books when they read such books on their own. Assigning a book is not the same as teaching a book. When too much assigning and not enough teaching occurs, students are on the road to readicide.

Reversing the Trend

Realizing that neither chopping up books nor handing students a classic and wishing them good luck are the way to get students to read deeply, teachers must constantly search for the sweet spot of just enough reading instruction. To help find this balance, I ask myself as I assign texts,

How much do my kids need me at this juncture of reading? How much support would be too much right now—or not enough?

One thing I have learned is that students need most of my help up-front, often before they even begin reading the text. To understand why, read the following passage:

> The pitcher's stuff was filthy. He was bringing cheese. He mixed in some chin music. Along with the heat, Uncle Charlie would occasionally show his face, producing a number of bowel-lockers. Only two batters got a knock. No one came close to dialing 8. (Gallagher, 2009, p. 95)

You probably understood every word in the above passage, but I am guessing that unless you know baseball well, you had a tough time comprehending it. Your inability to understand the passage is not a phonemic awareness problem, a fluency problem, or a vocabulary problem. You can read the words; you just lack the proper prior knowledge to make meaning.

Many students have this problem when approaching a difficult text, be it a primary source document or a Shakespeare play. This is where teaching (as opposed to assigning) becomes crucial; students need a teacher to supply the context. Before reading Chapter 1 of *To Kill a Mockingbird*, for instance, students should have an understanding of Herbert Hoover, the Great Depression, the Scottsboro Case (which inspired Harper Lee to write the novel), and the kind of racism that existed in the U.S. South at the time. On a more concrete level, many of my students do not know what a veranda is. They need vocabulary support before reading Lee's classic.

This kind of framing, however, is not in itself enough to generate the level of motivation required for my students to tackle a classic. Students today need more than history recaps and vocabulary lessons; they need to have some idea from the start of what they will gain from reading a text. I don't teach *To Kill a Mockingbird* because it's a great book. I teach *To Kill a Mockingbird* because it's a great book that puts my students in a place where they can examine racism today.

In a similar vein, when I teach *1984*, it doesn't overly concern me that some of my students are not going to like the novel. What concerns me is that all my students understand the value of the reading experience. As they read George Orwell's classic, I want my students to gain awareness of government surveillance today. I want them to understand that the torture site "Room 101" is not simply limited to Orwell's world—that many believe it has been recreated in Abu Ghraib and the detention center at Guantanamo Bay, Cuba. I want them to recognize the degree of language manipulation and propaganda they will confront for the rest of their lives. But I must make this value visible *before* my students commence reading. In introducing novels like these, I always address the central question my students bring to the book: Why should I care?

Before reading *Romeo and Juliet*, for example, I begin by having my students explore the question of whether long-term feuds can ever be buried. This question resonates with these learners, many of whom live in neighborhoods where gangs are a way of life. Although Shakespeare asked this question more than 400 years ago, it still holds value for the modern teenager. As the reading progresses and my students begin to connect with the play, I gradually release more of the meaning-making responsibility to them.

Promote Close Reading

A key element to finding this instructional sweet spot is teaching students to read closely. Teaching close reading is not the same as chopping up a book into so many pieces that it becomes unrecognizable. It is accomplished better by having students read large, uninterrupted chunks of text and then strategically having them return to key passages for second- or third-draft reading and thinking.

If the only reading our students do is "one-and-done" reading, they will never develop a critical reading lens. One cannot read James Madison's Federalist papers or Toni Morrison's *Beloved* once and reach a deep level of understanding. If we are to sharpen students' critical thinking, we need to require them to read longer chunks of text and commit to giving them more close reading practice.

Another important way to promote close reading is to bring reading for pleasure back into students' lives. Our intense focus on testing has brought an intense focus on academic reading, so that students have little exposure to reading for enjoyment in school. Many teachers have pushed aside recreational reading, which may be one reason that so few youth read for enjoyment on their own.

The lack of recreational reading has dire consequences. Brain researcher Maryanne Wolf (2007) has discussed "word poverty," noting that "by kindergarten a gap of 32 million words already separates some children in linguistically-impoverished homes from their more stimulated peers" (p. 20). If students are to have any chance to develop their vocabulary or build the background knowledge needed to become effective readers, they must develop recreational reading habits early in life. And reading habits are not built by handing students reading passages buried in test booklets.

Teachers and administrators who are squeezing recreational reading out of the day have forgotten an important finding: Students who read for fun have higher reading scores than students who rarely read for enjoyment (National Center for Education Statistics, 2005). I have never had a student receive a high SAT verbal score who was not a voracious reader. And I doubt that any student I run into on the street 20 years from now will thank me for helping him or her recognize symbolism in *The Scarlet Letter*. In fact, I'd be happier if that student wanted to discuss the contemporary book he or she was carrying.

Pulling Out of the "Reading Recession"

Thomas Friedman (2009) claims that recessions have historically been great times for opportunities to arise. With apologies to Friedman, may I suggest that the United States is in a reading recession. I believe that the critical thinkers we so desperately need will emerge from classrooms where teachers have eschewed the coverage approach in favor of fostering deeper thinking—and where the development of lifelong reading habits has remained as important as next month's test.

References

Cavanagh, S. (2009, March 11). "Depth" matters in high school science studies. *Education Week*, pp. 1, 16–17.

Dillon, S. (2009, October 30). Federal researchers find lower standards in schools. *The New York Times*, p. A22.

Friedman, T. (2009, June 28). Invent. Invent. Invent. *The New York Times*, p. WK8.

Gallagher, K. (2009). *Readicide*. Portland, ME: Stenhouse.

Gewertz, C. (2009, August 25). 2009 SAT scores declined or stagnated, college board reports. *Education Week*. Retrieved from www.edweek.org/ew/articles/2009/08/25/02sat.h29.html

National Center for Education Statistics. (2005). *National Assessment of Educational Progress*. Washington, DC: U.S. Department of Education.

National Council of Teachers of English. (2006). *NCTE principles of adolescent literacy reform: A public policy research brief*. Urbana, IL: Author.

National Endowment for the Arts. (2007). *To read or not to read: A question of national consequence* (Research Division Report 47). Washington, DC: Author.

Sternberg, R. (2007/2008). Assessing what matters. *Educational Leadership*, 65(4), 20–26.

Wolf, M. (2007). *Proust and the squid: The story and science of the reading brain*. New York: HarperCollins.

Kelly Gallagher (kellygallagher@cox.net) teaches English at Magnolia High School in Anaheim, California, and is the author of *Readicide* (Stenhouse, 2009).

Originally published in the March 2010 issue of *Educational Leadership*, 67(6): pp. 36–41.

Becoming a Classroom of Readers

Donalyn Miller

What makes students want to read?

As I stand in the hallway, monitoring students at their lockers before school begins, Emily wanders over to chat. She has been reading *Fever 1793* by Laurie Halse Anderson (Simon and Schuster, 2000), a historical fiction novel about the 1793 yellow fever epidemic in Philadelphia. The events in the book have piqued Emily's interest in medicine and epidemics.

Emily is full of questions. "Mrs. Miller, why did people back then have such weird ideas about diseases? Why did they drain people's blood and feed them nasty herbs to cure them? Didn't they know that mosquitoes caused yellow fever? Why do we know this now, but no one knew it then?"

"Well," I tell her, "scientists' study of infectious diseases like yellow fever has occurred over time, and years ago, we didn't know what caused many illnesses or how to treat them. There is a great nonfiction book called *An American Plague* by Jim Murphy (Clarion, 2003) that can give you more information about the 1793 yellow fever epidemic. Would you like to read it? We have a copy in the school library."

Emily agrees to read Murphy's book next and heads off to science class, where her newfound interest in infectious diseases will serve her well. During the 10 minutes between the first bell and the second, I discuss the Japanese invasion of Burma during World War II with Brian, who is reading Roland Smith's *Elephant Run* (Hyperion, 2007); debate the negative consequences of time travel explored in Rebecca Stead's *When You Reach Me* (Wendy Lamb, 2009) with Hanna; and define and pronounce *crenellated* for Grant, who declares that Christopher Paolini overuses the word in *Eragon* (Knopf, 2003). None of these students is in my first period language arts class, but their books provoke questions that cannot wait. As a reader, I enjoy these conversations, but as a teacher, I appreciate the intellectual power these students are gaining through reading.

The Need to Read

Numerous studies prove that wide reading improves children's comprehension, background knowledge, vocabulary, fluency, and writing (Krashen, 2004). Unfortunately, in many schools the poorest readers read the least, often as much as three times less than their peers (Allington, 2006). Many students identified as struggling readers early in their educations continue to receive reading intervention and tutoring throughout their school lives, never catching up with their peers. No matter what instructional methods we employ, students must spend substantial time applying the reading skills and strategies we teach before they develop reading proficiency. To become good readers, students must read and read and read.

The challenge for many teachers lies in motivating and inspiring students to pick up a book in the first place. Developing or struggling readers often lack the experience and confidence to choose books for themselves, read for extended periods of time, or consistently apply reading strategies across texts. Dormant readers, who possess the reading skills needed for academic tasks, see reading as a school job—not as an activity in which they would willingly engage outside school. How do we instill lasting reading behaviors in all our students?

Lifelong readers possess certain habits that we can explicitly model and teach our students. By redesigning our classrooms to support young readers as they practice and internalize the behaviors of avid readers, we can increase our students' engagement in reading and reap the benefits that prolific reading engenders.

Making Time

When I announce, "Ladies and gentlemen, come to a stopping spot," my students groan. Their complaints are music to my ears. I learned long ago that the only way I could guarantee that my students read was to dedicate time for them to read in class every day. The Commission on Reading's report *Becoming a Nation of Readers* (Anderson, Hiebert, Scott, & Wilkinson, 1985) recommends two hours of silent sustained reading a week, but increasing curriculum demands and the need to prepare students for standardized tests have made independent reading time a luxury in many classrooms. Knowing that voracious readers make time to read every day, how do we carve out more reading time for students?

I set aside as much as 30 minutes a day for my 6th grade students to read in class. During this time, I confer with students about the books they are reading, ask students to read to me while I assess their comprehension and fluency, and work with students in small groups.

If dedicating chunks of your instructional day for independent reading seems difficult, you can still find time for students to read more. In my own school, I realized that there was a lot of wasted time spent waiting in lines for picture day, field trips, the bus, and assemblies—time when my students could read. After all, adult readers carry books with us for those times when we must unexpectedly wait. We read at the airport, at the doctor's office, and on the train.

Teach students to carry a book wherever they go and to enjoy a few minutes of reading time. Those stolen moments add up over a year. Young readers learn what committed readers know— keeping a book with you alleviates boredom! My students have even learned to pull out their books whenever visitors at the door, phone calls, and technology glitches interrupt classroom instruction.

Maximizing wasted moments in the school day may garner as much as an hour each week of reading time for students, but we can allocate more reading time by eliminating warm-ups and "when you are done" activities. At a recent conference, I asked the crowd to identify the true purpose of warm-ups and bell ringers, those activities that we have ready for students to complete when they enter our classrooms. Embarrassed, most teachers admitted that these activities were designed so that they could take attendance or make sure students are working as soon as class begins.

Common warm-up activities in language arts classrooms, such as editing sentences, vocabulary study, or journal prompts, may yield limited instructional benefits; but none produce the same level of academic power as 15 minutes of reading time. The same could be said for "when you are done" activities and enrichment folders. I tell my students that they are never done: When they finish class work, they read. Students can gain as much as 20 minutes of extra reading in class each day when teachers designate reading as the only activity for any class time not used for instruction and practice.

Having time to read in class motivates my students to read more at home, too. Captivated by the books they're reading, they cannot wait until the next school day to continue their books. Recently, I received an e-mail from a mother who discovered the night before that her son had fallen asleep while reading Scott Westerfeld's newest science fiction epic, *Leviathan* (Simon Pulse, 2009).

Every morning and after school breaks, students swarm me to share how their love of reading seeps over into their personal lives.

As teachers and parents, we know that people who read when no one requires it are truly readers.

Giving Freedom

Although providing my students with more time to read dramatically increases the amount of reading they do, no single practice inspires my students to read as much as the opportunity to choose their own books. Learners who lack input into decision making feel powerless and unmotivated—this is true for adults, for teachers, and for our students (Cambourne, 1995).

We may spend weeks designing the perfect novel units, carefully selecting interesting texts and crafting meaningful activities, only to discover that our students merely plod through the book and our assignments. In addition, no one text or activity can possibly meet the needs of the diverse range of reading levels and interests found in the typical classroom.

So how can we accomplish our instructional goals and ensure that our students will be engaged? I have done away with whole-class novel units and allowed my students to choose their own books. A recent conversation I had with students about Suzanne Collins's futuristic novel *The Hunger Games* (Scholastic, 2008) confirmed my belief about whole-class novels. I never assigned *The Hunger Games* to my students, but after I mentioned it in book talks and offered it to my afterschool book club, the book's popularity spread like wildfire. Of my 93 students, almost 60 of them have read or plan to read this book.

When I asked one student, Adam, why this book was so popular, he told me, "You made the book sound so exciting, and I decided to read it because I thought I would be missing out. The book was amazing! I loved the action and terror of the Games, and I thought that Katniss [the protagonist] was a great character. When she volunteered to take her sister's place in the games, I thought it was so brave."

Curious, I asked, "Adam, knowing that this book is worth reading, with lots of topics we could discuss in class, what would you think about my assigning this book to the entire class? Most of you are reading it, anyway. Obviously, many students would enjoy it."

My question sparked a wave of head shaking and protests from Adam and his classmates who were discussing the book with us. "No, no, please don't! When teachers tell us we have to read a book, we hate it. We like it that we get to choose what we read." Even though I could use heartfelt recommendations, thought-provoking discussions, probing questions, and many other techniques I was using in book talks and small-group discussions when teaching a novel to the entire class, my students' reactions revealed that the most important factor for them was having the choice to read the book. (See Figure 6.1 for some of my students' favorite books.)

Options and Requirements

Asking some students to read devolves into a struggle to get them to pick up a book in the first place, so I don't provide students with the option of not reading. Instead, I ask students what book they *will* be reading today. I move the opportunity for choice to book selection. Allowing students to choose what they will read gives them power and removes the opportunity to refuse to read at all. That will be enough to motivate some students.

I require my students to read 40 books each year, in a mix of genres from nonfiction to fiction to poetry. Requiring my students to read widely exposes them to more genres, authors, vocabulary, and background knowledge than I could ever accomplish by teaching a few texts each year; and it helps students discover and develop their own reading tastes.

My instruction is focused on the knowledge and skills students must learn to meet state and district requirements. All students learn how to infer a book's themes, predict resolutions, identify figurative

Figure 6.1: Our 15 Favorite Books

Chosen by Donalyn Miller's 6th Grade Classes

Diary of a Wimpy Kid by Jeff Kinney (Diary of a Wimpy Kid series; Amulet, 2007). Greg Heffley, loser/hero, records his triumphs and trials while navigating the harsh world of middle school. Kinney's childlike cartoons enhance Greg's story.

Found by Margaret Peterson Haddix (Simon and Schuster, 2008). When Chip and Jonah receive cryptic letters in the mail, the boys embark on an investigation to uncover the secret surrounding their mysterious adoptions 13 years before. Also recommended is the sequel, *Sent* (Simon and Schuster, 2009).

Gone by Michael Grant (HarperTeen, 2008). In Perdido Beach, Florida, life is normal (mostly) until a sudden disruption results in the disappearance of every person over 15. Left to fend for themselves without computers, cell phones, or television, the remaining children must band together to survive. Also recommended is the sequel, *Hunger* (Harper-Teen, 2009).

Heat by Mike Lupica (Philomel, 2006). The star pitcher on his Little League team, Michael hides his father's death and his illegal immigrant status so he can continue to play the game.

The Hunger Games by Suzanne Collins (Scholastic, 2008). Welcome to Panem, a postapocalyptic United States. As punishment for the rebellion that led to war, each of 12 districts must send tributes to compete in the Hunger Games. One boy and one girl, chosen by lottery, must fight the other competitors to the death until only one remains. Also recommended is the sequel, *Catching Fire* (Scholastic, 2009).

Leviathan by Scott Westerfeld (Simon Pulse, 2009). World War I is reimagined as a clash between the Clankers, who rely on elaborate war machines, and the Darwinists, who craft weaponry from biologically engineered animals. Keith Thompson's elaborate black-and-white illustrations bring Westerfeld's steampunk world to life.

The Lightning Thief by Rick Riordan (Percy Jackson and the Olympians series; Hyperion, 2005). Bounced out of six schools in six years and diagnosed with ADHD, Percy Jackson finds out that he is really a demigod, descended from the Olympians of Greek mythology.

The London Eye Mystery by Siobhan Dowd (David Fickling, 2009). Ted, a young man with Asperger's syndrome and a fondness for weather forecasts, works with his older sister, Kat, to find their cousin, Salim, who has disappeard while riding the London Eye observation wheel.

continued

> **Figure 6.1: Our 15 Favorite Books** (*continued*)
>
> **Masterpiece** by Elise Broach (Henry Holt, 2008). James Pompaday, a lonely 11-year-old boy, discovers a new friend in Marvin, a beetle who lives under the kitchen sink. After Marvin creates a marvelous drawing using James's pen and ink set, the two friends embark on an adventure to trap art forgers at the Metropolitan Museum of Art.
>
> **The Maze of Bones** by Rick Riordan (The 39 Clues series; Scholastic, 2008). When Gracie Cahill, the last matriarch of the Cahill family, dies, her will challenges her heirs to uncover the 39 clues that will reveal the source of the family's power. Each installment in the series is written by a well-known children's author.
>
> **The Maze Runner** by James Dashner (Delacorte, 2009). Thomas, deprived of all memories except his name, is trapped in the Glade, a community surrounded by an ever-changing maze. Thomas works with the other Gladers to find an escape route and an explanation for their imprisonment.
>
> **NERDS: National Espionage, Rescue, and Defense Society** by Michael Buckley (Amulet, 2009). Six unpopular but brilliant elementary school students turn their nerdy qualities into assets with technological enhancements. Using a secret spy base hidden inside their school, the NERDS fight evil geniuses around the globe.
>
> **Peak** by Roland Smith (Harcourt, 2007). After he is arrested for climbing and tagging skyscrapers, Peak Marcelo must live with his estranged father, a professional mountain climber who leads expeditions up Mount Everest.
>
> **Stormbreaker** by Anthony Horowitz (Alex Rider series; Philomel, 2001). When his uncle (and guardian) is killed in a supposed car accident, Alex Rider discovers that his uncle was an M16 agent. Reluctantly recruited by the agency, Alex attempts to find his uncle's killers and complete his final mission.
>
> **When You Reach Me** by Rebecca Stead (Wendy Lamb, 2009). Obsessed with *A Wrinkle in Time* and helping her mom win a spot on *The $20,000 Pyramid*, Miranda suddenly sees her life grow more complicated when she receives mysterious notes that eerily predict her future.

language, and so on, but each student chooses his or her own books to practice and perfect these skills.

For students who lack reading experience and confidence in choosing books, I introduce a wide range of books and authors through readalouds and shared reading, where all students follow along as I read. Shared reading provides support for developing readers because the teacher scaffolds texts that students may not be able to read on their own. By following a more fluent reader, students can focus on comprehension instead of decoding. Students frequently seek out books and authors that we share in class. I often use the first chapter of a book as a teaching piece, then place the book on the chalkboard rail for students to enjoy. The book rarely lasts the day before a student checks it out to read.

When students select books on their own, I condone their choices. Books like the Diary of a Wimpy Kid series and the Bone graphic novels are popular with young readers, but teachers often denounce such books because they are short, are said to lack literary merit, or contain too many pictures. But consider that any girl who reads the entire Twilight series has read over a thousand pages of text. Surely, this is a powerful reading accomplishment! I celebrate any reading my students do.

When students see that I value their reading choices, they begin to trust themselves to select their own reading material and trust me to suggest more books. I tap into this relationship to move students toward more challenging, meatier books over time. For example, when I noticed that Shayla loved books about animals, particularly horses and dogs, I used her interest in Laurie Halse Anderson's Vet Volunteers series to suggest more challenging books like Anna Sewell's classic *Black Beauty*.

I work closely with students who struggle to select books or commit to a reading plan; I help them set short-term goals, such as reading so many pages per week or finishing one book. I encourage and praise these students for every step they take toward their reading goals. For students who resist trying anything, I have assigned a book as a last resort, choosing a title that I think the student might like and be able to read.

The Gift of Reading

The more students read, the better readers they become. By dedicating reading time, recommending books, exposing students to a variety of texts and authors, and validating their reading choices, I've seen students' interest and motivation to read increase. Students' background knowledge, understanding of text structure and features, vocabulary usage, appreciation for authors' craft, and performance on a wide array of assessments improve tremendously because of the reading they do. For it is only through volumes and volumes of reading that many students internalize the comprehension skills and gain the reading experience they must acquire for academic success.

Of course, hours and hours spent reading and the freedom to choose their own books also leads many children to discover a love of books and reading—a path to enjoyment and learning that lasts long after schooling ends. This is an immeasurable gift.

References

Allington, R. (2006). *What really matters for struggling readers: Designing research-based programs.* Boston: Pearson.

Anderson, R. C., Hiebert, E. H., Scott, J. A., & Wilkinson, I. A. G. (1985). *Becoming a nation of readers: The report of the Commission on Reading.* Washington, DC: National Institute of Education.

Cambourne, B. (1995). Toward an educationally relevant theory of literacy learning: Twenty years of inquiry. *The Reading Teacher, 49*(3), 182–190.

Krashen, S. (2004). *The power of reading: Insights from the research.* Portsmouth, NH: Heinemann.

Donalyn Miller (thebookwhisperer@gmail.com) teaches 6th grade language arts at Trinity Meadows Intermediate School in Bedford, Texas. She is the author of *The Book Whisperer: Awakening the Inner Reader in Every Child* (Jossey-Bass, 2009).

Originally published in the March 2010 issue of *Educational Leadership, 67*(6): pp. 30–35.

Unlocking the Secrets of Complex Text

Mary Ehrenworth

How to teach students to discover multiple meanings in the nonfiction they read.

If you ever find yourself at a live baseball game with a dominant pitcher, you might experience one of those evenings in which you see no runs or even hits. Such games cause baseball enthusiasts to exult, and they drive the rest of the population into a torpid boredom. To the experienced "reader" of baseball, who is alert to what is happening on the field as well in the batter's box, a shutout game is full of intricacy and drama, crucial decisions, and debatable moments. To the novice baseball reader, it's a game in which nothing happens.

We want students to be positioned to read complex nonfiction the way the expert reader of baseball reads the game—staying alert to the nuances and challenges of complex texts, to the reading work such texts demand, and to how they reward close reading (or whatever you want to call such alert, attentive reading). "Like any other art, craft, or sport, reading becomes more rewarding as we master its intricacies to higher degrees," writes Robert Scholes (1989, p. 18). Scholes suggests that texts release their secrets to those who come ready to see more.

Our job is to instill in students a deep sense of engagement with the intricacies of complex texts, to rouse them to see more in the texts they read—and to do this in a way that makes them want to read more. That means that readers need to feel their work paying off. Threatening them with hard state tests or future tasks in high school or college is not an effective teaching methodology (even if students will face these challenges). You can't discipline students into becoming insightful.

John Dewey (1909/1975) asks, "Who can reckon up the loss of moral power that arises from the constant impression that nothing is worth doing in itself, but only as a preparation for something else?" (p. 25). More recently, Timothy Shanahan (2013) notes that although many versions of close reading have been espoused in the wake of the Common Core State Standards, we need to remember that close reading is an outcome, not a technique.

The truth is, learning to see more in dense and complicated texts is an end in itself. Discernment, perception, and heightened awareness all bring heightened pleasure.

This close reading work will pay off most, of course, on real texts, such as Dr. Martin Luther King Jr.'s speeches. It probably won't pay off on textbooks that are already summaries, or on tiny nonfiction excerpts. It will pay off most on texts that kids find inherently fascinating (Allington & Gabriel, 2012); that seem relevant to the identities they are building (Tatum, 2005); and that they are reading for real reasons (Duke & Pearson, 2002). That might mean periodicals such as *Ranger Rick*, *Junior Scholastic*, or *Upfront Magazine*. It might mean science trade books by Gail Gibbons, Seymour Simon, or Brian Greene. It might mean videos by Nova, National Geographic, or Ken Burns. That is, real texts that real people read for knowledge and pleasure.

Hattie's research (2011) suggests that when you want to accelerate students' progress toward a goal, it helps if they have a clear vision of what they are trying to achieve. The following close-reading practices will promote such a vision.

Reading for Multiple and Implicit Ideas

When we teach students to expect that most texts are about more than one thing, we lead them to read more closely. It's also helpful to alert students that a lot of the nonfiction they read won't make every idea explicit through a heading or subheading, so they need to read for underlying, implicit ideas as well as explicit, surface ones.

To get students to read this way, first choose a text that will reward this work. You're looking for text that is *accessible, engaging,* and *complex*: *accessible* because if you introduce new, hard thinking work using new, hard texts, kids will struggle on all fronts; *engaging* because if students are engaged, they're willing to work hard; and *complex* so that if they do the work, it pays off—they gain new insights and epiphanies. The act of personally deriving new understandings produces intellectual and physical satisfaction; it actually releases endorphins into the brain (Rock, 2007).

To create opportunities for these epiphanies, you'll have to look at possible texts and sort out the difference between *difficult* and *complex*. A textbook might be difficult, but it might not be sufficiently complex if it has already laid out the thinking work for its readers. A high-quality nonfiction trade book, on the other hand, might seem easier at first glance, but if it's well-written and conveys multiple ideas, its complexity will reward close reading. Our job is to teach readers to expect to do this thinking work. The book's job is to make it rewarding.

For instance, take *Shark Attack!* by Cathy Dubowski (Dorling Kindersley, 2009), a nonfiction text that moves back and forth from narrative to exposition. It starts out with the true story of Rodney Fox, who was attacked by a great white shark while spearfishing in Australian waters. The first chapter presents Rodney's struggle with the shark as he is first bitten, then nearly swallowed, then dragged into the deep.

It's a gory, Homeric epic. Through it all, Rodney fights back, eventually making it to the surface damaged but alive.

After that harrowing tale, *Shark Attack!* offers facts about different species of sharks, especially the ones that are "really dangerous" (p. 15). Then it offers another true account of a shark following his victim up onto the sands of an Australian beach, where the shark savages the swimmer as six lifeguards wrestle with it. And in case you would consider ever swimming again, you next read about a bull shark that made its way into a freshwater creek in New Jersey. (Nothing good happens there, either.)

As the book moves from narrative to expository text, it also moves from an ominous tone to an oddly cheerful one (as you find out about handy shark repellent and protective metal cages) that's somehow even more chilling. It's the kind of fascinating and horrifying book you'd find on many shelves for young readers, alongside the eagerly read books on weather disasters, venomous snakes, and lethal insects—books that get kids interested in nonfiction by terrifying them. It's also the kind of complex nonfiction—full of dense information, implicit ideas, and multiple perspectives—that will reward close reading.

To do this reading work, first identify the book's central idea—that sharks are dangerous. It doesn't take much reading work for students to recognize that idea, so don't name that as close reading. To teach students to work harder and see more, you have to transform their expectations. You might say something like, "Chances are that this book, like so many, teaches more than one thing, and some of those things may not be obvious at first. The question readers ask themselves is, 'What else does this text teach?'"

Even though your teaching point aims to be transferable across texts, your demonstration needs to be specific so that students see what close-reading work actually looks like and realize that it's worth it to read this way. So next, do a bit of a demonstration that is specific to the text. In *Shark Attack!*, for instance, you might demonstrate how you could return to the account of the New Jersey creek attack and think aloud that although it's true that this section teaches that sharks are dangerous, it also suggests that people often help each other when there's danger. Leave room for students to build on your work, saying something like, "I wonder whether that idea runs through any other parts of the book—whether any other details support it? Hmm … and what other ideas does this book suggest?" The feeling in the room will be that you are coauthoring this work with your students. But you're also shifting their expectations of what it means to think as you read.

Then you want to give kids a chance to practice in your shared, familiar text. When they try reading this way in *Shark Attack!*, young readers tend to articulate implicit ideas like, "It's true that it teaches sharks are dangerous, but it also shows that you can survive shark attacks—that people can be tough." Whatever ideas students propose, you want to pose two questions: "What in the text makes you say that?" and "What other ideas does the text suggest? What details support those ideas?"

You'll probably want to offer this instruction in a mini-lesson, in which you do some shared reading of parts of a text that you've already introduced through a read-aloud (Calkins, 2010). That way students can work on close reading instead of working on initial comprehension. You might return to certain pages of the book by flipping through them on a document camera, showing them on an interactive smartboard, or giving kids copies to share. You might model how you look back over some pages, pushing yourself to name more than one idea by reconsidering what the stories, illustrations, lists, charts, and statistics teach (Calkins & Tolan, 2010). Then turn to other pages and invite students to give it a try.

Developing Structures for Transference

Chances are, if a teacher does the work described above using instructional read-alouds and shared reading, the teacher and the students will discern more than one idea about sharks and humans. But if that's all that happens, students may not realize that the reading work they did was transferable. They'll think it was *Shark Attack!* work.

One method to increase transference is to pay attention to the language you use as you're teaching and to consistently refer to the students' reading experiences outside the shared text. Use such phrases as, "Just like the nonfiction books you're reading independently, this book probably has more than one central idea," and "Whatever you're reading, I bet you're learning more than one thing."

You can also shorten the time between when students do this work with a teacher and when they try it out on other texts. Invite kids to bring the texts they are reading independently to the mini-lesson, and say,

> You know, this is not just *Shark Attack!* work. This should pay off in the other books or articles you're reading. So right now, get your book or article out. First, remind yourself of what you've been reading, and tell your partner one big idea your text is teaching. Then, go back to the text and see if you can find *another* idea the text suggests. Put your finger on the place where you realized the text was suggesting that new idea, and then argue your point quickly with your partner. Show what details in the text support your idea.

One more structure that will aid transference is the opportunity for repeated practice on a variety of texts, with calibrated feedback along the way. Hattie (2011) found that feedback in the midst of work, followed by the chance to put that feedback into play, dramatically improves student achievement. You should therefore ask yourself, Once I teach this, where in the curriculum will students get a chance to keep working on it? In middle and high school, that undoubtedly means planning curriculum strategically across the disciplines.

Analyzing Craft

As readers learn to ask themselves what a text is teaching them, we also want them to analyze *how* the text is teaching them. One way to do this work is to trace not only the ideas the text suggests but also the emotional response of the reader and what causes it. Reading is transactional—the text has an effect on the reader, and the alert reader pays attention to his or her response (Rosenblatt, 1982).

When you introduce this work, choose a text in which the emotional response is quite visceral so that readers get a sense of what it feels like to actively respond to nonfiction. Young readers who do this work on *Shark Attack!*, for instance, will often say that the book instills feelings of fear and tension. When you ask them to analyze what causes that fear, they may begin by noting the illustrations, especially those indelible images of Rodney caught in the shark's jaws. Some will also say it's the stories of horrific attacks. Some will note the shocking statistics. If you give students a chance to go back to the text and look closely at parts of it again, looking for the writer's craft, they'll often notice the capital letters, violent language, and exclamatory grammar: "Shark attack!" "CRASH!" "SNAP!" (pp. 4–9).

Here, you are teaching students that there are predictable questions readers can ask as they read to get more out of their reading: What does this text teach me? What does it make me feel? When students read with these lenses, they'll begin to notice that nonfiction authors use persuasive techniques and literary devices to make their points and get their readers to care. So they can also ask themselves, What techniques or craft does the author employ? What effect do these techniques have?

Choosing texts that make the writer's craft visible will help students see how informational texts work. When adults read nonfiction, we read it with years of experience with lots of other texts in our minds, so it's easier for us to see what the author is doing. Kids are building that store of knowledge with each text they analyze and each task they set themselves.

Developing Critical Stances

Many kids, on the basis of years of learned belief, subscribe to the notion that nonfiction is true; fiction is not. Once again, your teaching is about shifting readers' expectations. You'll want to teach students that nonfiction is not just "the truth"; it's someone's perspective on the truth. Students can only come to this realization if you ensure that they have opportunities to read more than one text on a subject. (See Figure 7.1 for some ideas.)

Figure 7.1: Paired Texts on Shared Topics

To show students how different texts can give different perspectives on the same topic, have them compare these texts.

Gail Gibbons, *Snakes* (Holiday House, 2010)	Seymour Simon, *Snakes* (HarperCollins, 2007)
Gail Gibbons, *The Planets* (Holiday House, 2008)	Seymour Simon, *Our Solar System* (HarperCollins, 2007)
Gail Gibbons, *Planet Earth/Inside Out* (Harper Collins, 1998)	Seymour Simon, *Earth* (HarperCollins, 2003)
Kathy Dubowski, *Shark Attack!* (Dorling Kindersley, 2009)	Seymour Simon, *Sharks* (HarperCollins, 2006)
Joy Hakim, Chapter 15: Rosa Parks Was Tired in *History of Us: Since 1945* (Oxford University Press, 2008)	Howard Zinn, Chapter 5: "Black Revolt and Civil Rights," in *A Young People's History of the United States: Class Struggle to the War on Terror* (Seven Stories Press, 2007)
Paul Revere, *The Boston Massacre*, woodcut, 1770	Patrick Henry, "Give Me Liberty or Give Me Death," 1775
Dr. Martin Luther King Jr., "I Have a Dream," 1963	President John F. Kennedy, "Civil Rights Address," 1963

Note: For access to more nonfiction texts sets assembled around shared topics, see the Reading and Writing Project (http://readingandwritingproject.com/resources/classroom-libraries/text-sets.html), which lists digital nonfiction text sets offering multiple perspectives on disputed issues; Buzzle (www.buzzle.com), which offers accessible texts sifted by topic and issue; and Newspapermap (http://newspapermap.com), which provides access to front-page newspaper articles from around the globe.

As a starting point, assemble text sets that offer different perspectives on shared topics. For example, when you put Cathy Dubowski's *Shark Attack!* next to Seymour Simon's *Sharks* (HarperCollins, 2006), the content, craft, and perspective of each become more apparent. Or gather sources on some controversial topics, and then add to students' reading lenses questions such as those in Figure 7.2.

Ultimately, we want students to feel that they haven't really read about something if they've read only one text on the topic. We want them to actively seek out varied perspectives—to be dissatisfied with limited knowledge. We are educating them not for that state test, nor for that college class, but for the contributions they'll make to this world.

You may wonder whether teaching readers to question is reading instruction. That's really what reading is, though: a constant, quiet questioning of the text, of the reader's response, and of the meanings that emerge in this interaction. Questioning also includes the ability to reflect, to revise thinking, and to remain open to new ideas. When we teach readers to come to the text with a questioning attitude, we are teaching them to develop not only close-reading practices, but also intellectual stances.

Figure 7.2: Some Questions Readers Might Pose

Close Readers Might Begin by Asking These Questions:

- What does this text want me to know? What information does this text teach?
- What does this text want me to understand? What new ideas and concepts does it suggest?
- What does this text want me to feel? What emotions does it stir up?
- How does it accomplish these tasks?

Close and Critical Readers Might Then Ask These Questions:

- Whose perspective is represented in this text?
- Whose point of view is most fully explored?
- Who is honored or privileged in the text and how? Who is marginalized?
- How does the perspective in this text compare with others on this issue?
- How does the author use persuasive techniques, literary devices, or writerly craft to convey meaning?

Constructing Arguments

Another method that leads students to read nonfiction more closely is positioning reading work as the work of weighing and evaluating evidence for arguments students are deeply engaged in. When students are invited to research and debate authentic arguments—arguments about search and seizure, the legal drinking age, deployment of the atom bomb, nuclear energy, or whether the class should go to the zoo or the museum for the next field trip—they tend to research with a fierceness that you don't often see in school. You'll see them circling parts of articles, combing websites, replaying newscasts, and comparing and contrasting evidence.

Searching for the evidence that most clearly makes their point and that stirs up their audience is the real reading work here. Whether they are writing essays or letters, preparing speeches or panel presentations, or debating, teach students to be alert to juicy quotes—to notice when an author says something with such compelling language that they want to use his or her exact words. As they hone their own arguments, teach them to compare how authors use facts and statistics, and how they use stories as examples and also to stir up sympathy. Teach them to read closely for evidence and also for parts of the text where the author might serve as a mentor.

When students are composing compelling arguments, they have reasons to go back to the texts, to glean every possible detail that might be important, to compare sources, and to align with or reject points of view. They also have reasons to consider the other side so that they can better defend their own. They become more alert to detail and perspective in their reading. When you teach research-based argument, you teach students "what it means to be a citizen in a participatory democracy ... to become discriminating and credible, influential, and engaged" (Calkins, Ehrenworth, & Taranto, 2013).

Opportunities for Self-Directed Reading

A cautionary note: Keep in mind that you want to set kids up to work on their reading by doing a lot of reading. The goal of this reading work is not to produce kids who spend hours on a single page of text, poring over the language at the wordsmith level like postgraduate students in literary theory. They could end up like an athlete who spends a lot of time thinking about running but rarely runs.

After all, the goal of reading nonfiction is to learn, and the best way to do that is to read a lot. Allington's research (2012) shows that to grow as readers, kids need protected time to read, access to books they find fascinating, and expert instruction. So if your "expert instruction" slows down students' practices initially as you coach them to sharpen their vision, you'll want to then let them loose on lots of fresh texts. With experience, readers do begin to naturally see more as they read—just as that experienced reader of baseball naturally notices a lot during the game, because he or she is alert to what there is to pay attention to.

Transforming Reading Practices in a School

Finally, if you want to get this work going with students, you might want to start with the adults in the building. Choose a text you'll find engaging, and try out these close-reading practices together. You're much more likely, then, to get more transference across the curriculum, including more opportunities for students to practice this work. You're also likely to change the discourse around close reading, so that it becomes a discourse of hard work and beauty. For you are not setting out to tinker with kids' reading skills, adding a strategy here or there. You are setting out to transform their ideas about what it means to read.

References

Allington, R. L. (2012). *What really matters for struggling readers: Designing research-based programs* (3rd ed.). Boston: Allyn and Bacon.

Allington, R., & Gabriel, R. (2012). Every child, every day. *Educational Leadership, 69*(6), 10–15.

Calkins, L. (2010). *A guide to the reading workshop.* Portsmouth, NH: Heinemann.

Calkins, L., Ehrenworth, M., & Taranto, A. (2013). *Research-based argument essays.* Portsmouth, NH: Heinemann.

Calkins, L., & Tolan, K. (2010). *Navigating nonfiction in expository text.* Portsmouth, NH: Heinemann.

Dewey, J. (1909/1975). *Moral principles in education.* Carbondale: Southern Illinois University Press. (Original work published 1909)

Duke, N., & Pearson, D. (2002). Effective practices for developing reading comprehension. In S. J. Samuels & A. E. Farstrup (Eds.), *What research has to say about reading instruction* (3rd ed., pp. 205–242). Newark, DE: International Reading Association.

Hattie, J. (2011). *Visible learning for teachers: Maximizing impact on learning.* New York: Routledge.

Rosenblatt, L. (1982). The literary transaction: Evocation and response. *Theory into Practice, 21*(4), 268–277.

Rock, D. (2007). *Quiet leadership: Six steps to transforming performance at work.* New York: HarperBusiness.

Shanahan, T. (2013, March 24). Why discussions of close reading sound like nails scratching on a chalkboard [blog post]. Retrieved from *Shanahan on Literacy* at www.shanahanonliteracy.com/2013/03/why-discussions-of-close-reading-sounds_2091.html

Scholes, R. (1989). *Protocols of reading.* New Haven, CT: Yale University Press.

Tatum, A. (2005). *Teaching reading to black adolescent males: Closing the achievement gap.* Portland, ME: Stenhouse.

Mary Ehrenworth (maryehrenworth@post.harvard.edu) is deputy director of the Teachers College Reading and Writing Project, Columbia University, New York.

Originally published in the November 2013 issue of *Educational Leadership, 71*(3): pp. 16–21.

8

You Want Me to Read What?!

Timothy Shanahan

A sometimes tongue-in-cheek but always informative look at the questions surrounding the new emphasis on informational text.

> Common Core also shifts away from classic literature and allows for the reading of informational texts .... And what are informational texts? Those are handbooks from the EPA on how to make sure that your siding and your insulation is good in your house. Who in their right mind wants to read the government handbooks?
>
> —Glenn Beck (2013)

Who, indeed?

Surprisingly, the Common Core State Standards avoided becoming the piñata of the kinds of petty controversies that have been customary in past discussions of curriculum reform in English language arts. During the entire standards writing and adoption process, there were no "reading wars," no grandstanding governors emptily threatening to forego federal education support, no marching ministers or protesting pressure groups. All in all, it was a pretty civilized affair.

We're now in the implementation season, and things have heated up a bit, but the main arguments against the standards are more about issues like federalism, test policy, President Obama's education preferences, data mining, and so on (Strauss, 2013). Such complaints do not say much about whether these standards are any good.

For example, former Assistant Secretary of Education Diane Ravitch (2013) voiced a complaint that's pretty typical of the current reproaches:

> I have come to the conclusion that the Common Core standards effort is fundamentally flawed by the process with which they have been foisted upon the nation …. Maybe the standards will be great. Maybe they will be a disaster. Maybe they will improve achievement. Maybe they will widen the achievement gaps between haves and have-nots.

In other words, Ravitch avoids making claims about the value of the standards themselves but decries the standards adoption *process* instead.

But there has been one kind of criticism leveled against the new mandates—and it targets informational text. The new standards have asked for big increases in rigor and the level of instruction in reading, added prominence to a literary canon, proposed a shift from an emphasis on personal writing to one on academic writing, expanded literacy teaching into the disciplines of history and science, promoted deeper analysis of the ideas and arguments in texts, and placed a new emphasis on inquiry and 21st century research tools (National Governors Association Center for Best Practices [NGA] & Council of Chief State Schools Officers [CCSSO], 2010). Despite all those momentous changes, the major grumbles have been aimed at the fact that the standards encourage more reading of informational text at school.

In fairness, this will be an important change, and it's one that education leaders will have to think hard about if they're going to get it right. Here's my take on some of the key questions.

What Is Informational Text?

That's a good question and not one likely to generate much agreement. According to some treatments, informational text appears to be no more than a synonym for nonfiction (Brown & Schulten, 2012); in others, it describes only a portion of the nonfiction universe (Duke & Bennett-Armistead, 2003). According to the Common Core standards, literary nonfiction is a subpart of informational text (NGA & CCSSO, 2010); in other schemes, such as that used by the National Assessment of Educational Progress (NAEP), literary nonfiction isn't in the informational text basket at all (National Assessment Governing Board, 2010).

Probably the closest the standards come to defining informational text is within the writing standards, but that description, although helpful, differs in key ways from the concept presented in the reading standards. The writing standards define *informational/explanatory writing* as text that conveys information accurately "to increase readers' knowledge of a subject, to help readers better understand a procedure or process, or to provide readers with an enhanced comprehension of a concept" (NGA & CCSSO, 2010, p. 23). This definition goes on to explain that such writing addresses types and components; size, function, or behavior; how things work; and why things happen. In other words, the standards distinguish informational writing on the basis of its purposes and functions.

Unfortunately, in the reading standards, such texts are tossed into the informational text stewpot along with seemingly variant narrative and argumentative texts—a savory dish to be sure, yet quite different from the cuisine served up in the writing kitchen, where these ingredients are kept emphatically separated.

The testing consortia's takes on the concept retain some of this muddle. For example, in its discussion of reading complex texts for grade 7, the Partnership for Assessment of Readiness for College and Careers (PARCC) (2012) says that

> informational texts/literary nonfiction include the subgenres of exposition, argument, and functional text in the form of personal essays; speeches; opinion pieces; essays about art or literature; biographies; memoirs; journalism; and historical, scientific, technical, or economic accounts (including digital sources) written for a broad audience.

Similarly, the Smarter Balanced Assessment Consortium (2012) says that for grades 3–5, the category includes

> biographies and autobiographies; books about history, social studies, science, and the arts; technical texts, including directions, forms, and information displayed in graphs, charts, or maps; and digital sources on a range of topics.

And for grades 6–12, it includes

> the subgenres of exposition, argument, and functional text in the form of personal essays, speeches, opinion pieces, essays about art or literature, biographies, memoirs, journalism, and historical, scientific, technical, or economic accounts (including digital sources) written for a broad audience. (p. 8)

The problem is that these testing specifications conflate so many functions and text types that they confuse, and perhaps undermine, the whole point of distinguishing literary from informational texts in the first place. The idea is to ensure that students gain sufficient experience in dealing with the varied characteristics and demands of a wide range of texts. By including biographies or other "true stories" within the informational text category, narratives—both fact and fiction—can continue to dominate classroom instruction, narrowing the range of texts served up rather than ensuring a real expansion.

Obviously, there's nothing wrong with having students read true stories, but if they take the place of more explanatory or argumentative texts, then it vitiates the value of distinguishing between literary and informational text. Susan Pimentel, one of the chief authors of the standards, wrote,

> I think David [Coleman] and I have to take the blame for biographies and autobiographies and memoirs getting into the informational pile. To atone, we've been pushing hard on students reading informational text with informational text structures so as to counter the proclivity to just pick up another narrative that just happens to be true. (personal communication, October 16, 2012)

Ultimately, it doesn't really matter whether a biography is in the literary text pile (because it's a narrative) or in the informational one (because it's factual). What matters is that kids get a varied diet of text. School leaders have to push hard to ensure that classrooms go beyond fulfilling these categories nominally—that teachers select texts in a way that provides students with a sufficiently wide swath of reading experience.

Why are the standards making such a big deal out of informational text?

Studies have shown that elementary schools have done little to expose students to such texts (Duke, 2000) and that literary texts have dominated U.S. textbooks for a long time (Moss, 2008; Moss & Newton, 2002; Venezky, 1982; Watkins, 2011). That means that U.S. students read a lot of stories in their elementary classrooms, but not much science or history.

The concern is that such an unvaried reading diet can't possibly prepare students for the kinds of reading expected in college and the workplace. Devoting 80 percent of reading instruction to literature may improve students' performance in their English classes, but what about social studies, science, and math?

Does this imbalance affect students' reading achievement?

Maybe. According to the most recent international comparisons (Mullis, Martin, Foy, & Drucker, 2012), U.S. students don't read informational text as well as they read literary text. According to that study, there are nations where students read both kinds of text equally well and those where informational text performance is relatively higher.

In general, though, U.S. students did less well with informational text. Because the two kinds of text weren't scaled to be equally difficult, however, perhaps the informational texts used on the tests were relatively harder. Unfortunately, neither the NAEP nor the other international studies make such comparisons, so we can't say for sure that our students read one kind of text better than another.

Does research show that adding more informational text will improve student achievement?

No, not directly. No one has done a study to examine the learning results when students read different proportions of different kinds of text. The idea that students should get more experience reading informational text is based on the following commonsense notions:

- Because people read more informational texts in college and the workplace, it's important to become proficient with these texts.
- Strong evidence shows the differences between informational and literary texts as well as in the cognitive processes we use to read such texts (Otto, 1982; Weaver & Kintsch, 1991), so it follows that reading literary texts will not necessarily improve one's ability to handle informational texts.
- Students have much less experience reading informational text, which means less opportunity to learn how to read such texts well.

- People usually get better at what they practice, so if students had more chances to read informational text, they might improve their abilities in this area.

What should we expect students to learn from reading informational text?

Several years ago, I was talking to my wife and her aunt. I shared some arcane fact, and Auntie exclaimed, "He's smart!" My wife's immediate response? "No, he just reads a lot." And that's not a small thing.

E. D. Hirsch Jr. (2007) has long championed the importance of cultural knowledge, and research shows that comprehension is influenced by what we know (Kintsch, 1998). The most obvious outcome we can hope for is that students will end up knowing more about their social and natural world from reading informational texts—and that could have a positive effect on their reading comprehension.

In addition, informational text is usually organized differently from literary text. Informational text is more likely to use problem–solution, cause–effect, and compare–contrast rhetorical structures. And because of the way the standards categorize texts, argument would fall within its purview as well.

Text features differ, too. (When was the last time you saw bullet points in a poem?) Bold print, italics, headings and subheadings, and sidebars are all more common in informational text. Text guides such as tables of contents and indexes, for example, differ in important ways, as do illustrations and graphics and the roles they play. Of course, we read such texts for different purposes, and that makes us vary our reading approaches. Through reading and analyzing informational texts (and receiving explicit instruction), students should develop effective responses to all of these structures, features, and purposes.

But why can't English teachers teach "classical literature" anymore?

The Common Core standards proposed proportions of reading time that should be devoted to literary and informational texts in elementary and secondary schools: In elementary school, half the time should be spent on informational text; this should expand to 70 percent by middle school.

Many critics have misinterpreted this as a requirement that high school English teachers spend no more than 30 percent of their class time on poetry, short stories, novels, and plays. However, as the standards explicitly state,

> The percentages ... reflect the sum of student reading, not just reading in ELA [English language arts] settings. Teachers of senior English classes, for example, are not required to devote 70 percent of reading to informational texts. Rather, 70 percent of student reading across the grade should be informational. (NGA & CCSSO, 2010, p. 5)

Do the math. Under the new standards, English teachers will still be spending the lion's share of their time on literature, but that means that history, science, and math teachers need to have students reading appropriate texts in their classes, too.

Should English teachers be spending any time on informational text?

Yes. In a forthcoming national survey (Thomas B. Fordham Foundation, in press), which took place early on in the standards implementation process, high school English teachers claimed that 40 percent of students' current classroom reading already involved literary nonfiction and informational text.

English teachers are great guides to teaching informational text because they bring special tools to the table—they know how to analyze and interpret rhetoric and language. They have insights about reading that are valuable for dealing with essays, speeches, journalistic writing, and other literary nonfiction. So, along with lots of attention to stories and poems, some English class time is well spent on informational texts.

Does this mean that we'll be teaching fiberglass installation manuals and the minutes of Federal Reserve Board meetings?

I've pored over the lists of exemplary texts suggested by the standards, and I've not been able to find either of those entries. You might want to take a look yourself. Maybe these were considered, but they just didn't make the final cut.

What the Common Core standards have recommended are texts like Abraham Lincoln's "Gettysburg Address"; the U.S. Constitution; the Declaration of Independence; Winston Churchill's "Blood, Toil, Tears, and Sweat" speech; Ronald Reagan's speech to the students of Moscow University; and a plethora of texts on science and technology, including ones on space probes, elementary particles, architecture, and engineering. I'll keep my eyes peeled for the fiberglass installation manual, however.

My kindergarten teachers say that informational text is developmentally inappropriate for young children. Is that true?

This canard is definitely making the rounds. Some critics point out that informational text doesn't really reflect young children's developmental stages or interests.

I can't find any developmental psychologist willing to support such cautions, and the only person I could find willing to go on the record with an opinion on the subject was my nephew Dominic, age 7, who admittedly isn't an expert on these matters. Nevertheless, he assures me that his early enthusiasm for the news magazine *Time for Kids* hasn't held him back in his scholarly pursuits so far, a pattern of interest that he apparently shares with many of his age mates (Donovan, Smolkin, & Lomax, 2000). In fact, many of the authorities who recommend informational text are doing so, at least in part, in response to children's interests in such materials.

A Balanced Diet

Arguments against the wide use of informational text with students lack an evidentiary foundation and ignore the reading demands that students will face in college and the workplace. The argument for informational texts is not that students should read more information and less literature but that they surely should read more of both (Jago, 2013). Righting the current imbalance will simply require increases in the reading of information.

References

Beck, G. (2013, April 8). The whole story on Common Core. *GlennBeck.com*. Retrieved from www.glennbeck.com/2013/04/08/the-whole-story-on-common-core

Brown, A. C., & Schulten, K. (2012, December 13). Fiction or nonfiction? Considering the Common Core's emphasis on informational text [blog post]. Retrieved from *The Learning Network* at the *New York Times* at http://learning.blogs.nytimes.com/2012/12/13/fiction-or-nonfiction-considering-the-common-cores-emphasis-on-informational-text

Donovan, C. A., Smolkin, L. B., & Lomax, R. G. (2000). Beyond the independent-level text: Considering the reader-text match in first graders' self-selections during recreational reading. *Reading Psychology, 21*(4), 309–333.

Duke, N. K. (2000). 3.6 minutes per day: The scarcity of informational texts in first grade. *Reading Research Quarterly, 35*(2), 202–224.

Duke, N. K., & Bennett-Armistead, V. S. (2003). *Reading and writing informational text in the primary grades.* New York: Scholastic.

Hirsch, E. D., Jr. (2007). *The knowledge deficit: Closing the shocking education gap for American children.* New York: Mariner Books.

Jago, C. (2013, January 10). What English classes should look like in the Common Core era [blog post]. Retrieved from *The Answer Sheet* at the *Washington Post* at www.washingtonpost.com/blogs/answer-sheet/wp/2013/01/10/what-english-classes-should-look-like-in-common-core-era

Kintsch, W. (1998). *Comprehension: A paradigm for cognition.* New York: Cambridge University Press.

Moss, B. (2008). The information text gap: The mismatch between non-narrative text types in basal readers and 2009 NAEP recommended guidelines. *Journal of Literacy Research, 40*(2), 201–219.

Moss, B., & Newton, E. (2002). An examination of the informational text genre in basal readers. *Reading Psychology, 23*(1), 1–13.

Mullis, I. V. S., Martin, M. O., Foy, P., & Drucker, K. T. (2012). *PIRLS 2011 international results in reading.* Chestnut Hill, MA: TIMSS & PIRLS International Study Center, Boston College.

National Assessment Governing Board. (2010). *Reading framework for the 2011 National Assessment of Educational Progress.* Washington, DC: Author.

National Governors Association Center for Best Practices & Council of Chief State School Officers. (2010). *Common Core State Standards for English language arts and literacy in history/social studies, science, and technical subjects.* Washington, DC: Author. Retrieved from www.corestandards.org/assets/ELA%20Standards.pdf

Otto, W. (Ed.). (1982). *Reading expository material.* New York: Academic Press.

Partnership for Assessment of Readiness for College and Careers. (2012). *Structure of the model content frameworks for ELA/reading.* Washington, DC: Author. Retrieved from www.parcconline.org/mcf/english-language-artsliteracy/structure-model-content-frameworks-elaliteracy

Ravitch, D. (2013, February 26). Why I cannot support the Common Core Standards [blog post]. Retrieved from *Diane Ravitch's Blog* at http://dianeravitch.net/2013/02/26/why-i-cannot-support-the-common-core-standards

Smarter Balanced Assessment Consortium. (2012). *Smarter Balanced Assessment Consortium: English language arts and literacy stimulus specifications.* Retrieved from author at www.smarterbalanced.org/wordpress/wp-content/uploads/2012/05/TaskItemSpecifications/EnglishLanguageArtsLiteracy/ELAStimulusSpecifications.pdf

Strauss, V. (2013, April 19). Common Core Standards attacked by Republicans. Retrieved from *The Answer Sheet* at the *Washington Post* at www.washingtonpost.com/blogs/answer-sheet/wp/2013/04/19/common-core-standards-attacked-by-republicans

Thomas B. Fordham Foundation. (in press). *National survey of English language arts and reading teachers at key grade levels.* Washington, DC: Author.

Venezky, R. L. (1982). The origins of the present-day chasm between adult literacy needs and school literacy instruction. *Visible Language, 16*(2), 113–126.

Watkins, N. M. (2011). *Examining text types in adolescent literature anthologies.* Unpublished doctoral dissertation, University of Utah.

Weaver, C. A., & Kintsch, W. (1991). Expository text. In R. Barr, M. L. Kamil, P. Mosenthal, & P. D. Pearson (Eds.), *Handbook of reading research* (Vol. 2, pp. 230–245). Hillsdale, NJ: Erlbaum.

Timothy Shanahan (shanahan@uic.edu) is distinguished professor of urban education, director of the Center for Literacy, and chair of the Department of Curriculum and Instruction at the University of Illinois, Chicago.

Originally published in the November 2013 issue of *Educational Leadership*, 71(3): pp. 10–15.

Closing in on Close Reading

Nancy Boyles

We can't wait until middle school to teach students to read closely. Three practices bring close reading to the lower grades.

A significant body of research links the close reading of complex text—whether the student is a struggling reader or advanced—to significant gains in reading proficiency and finds close reading to be a key component of college and career readiness. (Partnership for Assessment of Readiness for College and Careers, 2011, p. 7)

When I read this statement in the content frameworks of one of the consortia now creating assessments for the Common Core State Standards, I was frankly a little insulted. *Of course* I teach students to read closely—both my university students and younger students, through my literacy consultant work. But on closer examination, I realized I may not be encouraging students to read closely enough to meet the expectations set by these standards. Exactly what do the Common Core standards mean by close reading? And what principles and practices should guide us as we implement close reading in the classroom—particularly in elementary classrooms?

Much of the available information about close reading centers on secondary schools, where this skill seems to fit most comfortably. By the time students are in these later grades, they are more inclined to think abstractly. They read complicated texts by great authors that beg for careful analysis. But close reading can't wait until 7th grade or junior year in high school. It needs to find its niche in kindergarten and the years just beyond if we mean to build the habits of mind that will lead all students to deep understanding of text.

What Is Close Reading?

Essentially, close reading means reading to uncover layers of meaning that lead to deep comprehension. The Partnership for Assessment of Readiness for College and Careers (PARCC) supplies clarification useful for teaching with Common Core standards in mind:

> Close, analytic reading stresses engaging with a text of sufficient complexity directly and examining meaning thoroughly and methodically, encouraging students to read and reread deliberately. Directing student attention on the text itself empowers students to understand the central ideas and key supporting details. It also enables students to reflect on the meanings of individual words and sentences; the order in which sentences unfold; and the development of ideas over the course of the text, which ultimately leads students to arrive at an understanding of the text as a whole. (PARCC, 2011, p. 7)

If reading closely is the most effective way to achieve deep comprehension, then that's how we should teach students to read. But that description doesn't match much of the instruction I've witnessed in recent years.

Why Close Reading Now?

I wear a variety of professional hats—university professor, literacy consultant to districts, author of several books related to comprehension. To keep myself honest (and humble), I spend a lot of time in classrooms watching kids and teachers at work. During the past decade, I've observed a transformation in the teaching of reading from an approach that measured readers' successful understanding of text through lengthy packets of comprehension questions to one that requires students to think about their thinking, activating their "good reader" strategies. The National Assessment of Educational Progress even made one of those strategies—making reader/text connections—a thinking strand within its framework (National Assessment Governing Board, 2002). For a long while, this approach looked ideal. What could be better than creating metacognitive readers?

But the teaching of reading veered significantly off track when those personal connections (also well represented on some high-stakes state assessments) began to dominate the teaching and testing of comprehension, often leaving the text itself a distant memory. And it got even crazier. I wish I could say that the time I overheard a teacher say, "If you don't have a real connection, make one up" was an isolated incident.

Although well-intentioned, the shift to teaching reading as a set of thinking strategies too often left readers with the notion that the text was simply a launching point for their musings, images that popped into their heads, and random questions that, in the end, did little to enhance their understanding of the text itself.

So if responding personally to text isn't leading students to deeper understanding, then where should teachers turn to help students improve their comprehension? We should turn to the text itself.

Enter close reading.

Reread that PARCC definition of close reading—closely—to extract key concepts. You might identify these ideas: examining meaning thoroughly and analytically; directing attention to the text, central ideas, and supporting details; reflecting on meanings of individual words and sentences; and developing ideas over the course of the text. Notice that reader reflection is still integral to the process. But close reading goes beyond that: The best thinkers do monitor and assess their thinking, but in the context of processing the thinking of others (Paul & Elder, 2008).

Great, you may be thinking. I reread that passage. I processed. I monitored. And I agree that close reading will likely produce deeper understanding. But how do I get these concepts off the page and into my elementary school classroom? Here are three fruitful practices.

Use Short Texts

Most teachers subscribe to the belief that when students can read longer text, that's what they should read. Although we don't want to abandon longer texts, we should recognize that studying short texts is especially helpful if we want to enable students with a wide range of reading levels to practice closely reading demanding texts (Coleman & Pimentel, 2012).

The Common Core standards suggest several genres of short text, both literary and informational, that can work at the elementary level. Many kinds of traditional literature—folktales, legends, myths, fables, as well as short stories, poetry, and scenes from plays—enable and reward close reading. For informational works, try short articles, biographies, personal narratives, and even some easier primary-source materials, such as Martin Luther King Jr.'s "I Have a Dream" speech, the preamble to the U.S. Constitution, or sayings from *Poor Richard's Almanac*. Appendix B of the Common Core State Standards notes numerous picture books that can be used with younger readers. Because children's listening comprehension outpaces their reading comprehension in the early grades, it's important that your students build knowledge through being read to as well as through independent reading, with the balance gradually shifting to silent, independent reading.

When students are learning a process, such as how to search for a recurring theme, reading short texts allows them to make more passes through the entire sequence of a text. It could take weeks or even months to read through a 100-page novel to identify a theme or concepts related to the text as a whole. A short text of a page or two can be digested in one lesson.

Aim for Independence

Go Beyond "Ho-Hum" Questions

It's our responsibility as educators to build students' capacity for *independently* comprehending a text through close reading. There's some controversy, however, as to how we should go about doing this.

One organization, Student Achievement Partners—until recently led by David Coleman, a lead author of the Common Core standards—suggests that we accomplish this through "text-dependent questions." Coleman and colleagues (Coleman & Pimentel, 2012) advocate asking a sequence of questions that will lead students more deeply into a text. As an example, the organization's website presents this series of questions for 3rd graders, referring to the equivalent of 11 very sparse pages taken from Chapters 6 and 7 of Kate DiCamillo's novel *Because of Winn-Dixie* (Candlewick, 2000):

- Why was Miss Franny so scared by Winn-Dixie? Why was she "acting all embarrassed"?
- How did the Herman W. Block Memorial Library get its name?
- Opal says, "She looked sad and old and wrinkled." What happened to cause Miss Franny to look this way?
- What were Opal's feelings when she realized how Miss Franny felt?
- Earlier in the story, Opal says that Winn-Dixie "has a large heart, too." What does Winn-Dixie do to show that he has a "large heart"?

- Opal and Miss Franny have three very important things in common. What are these? (Student Achievement Partners, 2012)

The culminating task for this exemplar activity is to explain in writing why *Because of Winn-Dixie* is an appropriate title.

These are decent questions, requiring both literal and inferential thinking, but they fall short in several ways. First, none of them will generate real discussion; they all have basically a right answer, even those that don't call for verbatim "facts" from the story. Second, they are fairly ho-hum as questions go, sticking closely to the kinds of things we typically ask young readers. And asking students to justify a title when they have 19 more chapters to read seems a bit premature if you're looking for deep thinking based on the best evidence.

Most of these questions align only with Common Core English Language Arts and Literacy Anchor Standard 1: finding evidence in the text. A couple of the questions address characters' feelings (Standard 3); and the last question delves into the author's message (Standard 2). But we didn't need the Common Core standards to push us to ask questions like these. Teachers are already quite good at asking questions about *what* the author is saying.

Entirely missing from this question set is anything related to craft and structure (Standards 4–6) and integration of knowledge and ideas (Standards 7–9)—areas that are so often neglected, as the developers of the standards acknowledge. I would probe 3rd graders' thinking with questions like these:

- In these chapters, the author repeats a few phrases, like, "My daddy was a rich man, a very rich man." Why does the author do this? Find more repeated phrases. What effect do these have on the meaning of the story? (Standard 4: the use of language)
- In Chapter 7, Miss Franny Block tells Opal the story of the bear from long ago. Why do you think the author stops the action of the story to go back in time like this? What might not

have happened if Franny Block hadn't told this story? (Standard 5: text structure)
- What is Franny Block's point of view about Winn-Dixie by the end of Chapter 7? What is the evidence? Where does her point of view change? (Standard 6: point of view)

Questions related to the integration of knowledge and ideas might be better posed later in the book, after students have digested more of the text's content. But the craft and structure questions I've suggested could be asked at any time—and they get much closer to the range of rigor to which the Common Core standards aspire.

The final, most compelling reason I don't care for the Student Achievement Partners questions is that although they teach the reading—the content of the text—there's no attempt to teach the reader strategies by which that reader can pursue meaning independently, yes independently (notice my repetition for emphasis modeled after *Because of Winn-Dixie*).

Teach Students to Ask the Questions

Teaching is about transfer. The goal is for students to take what they learn from the study of one text and apply it to the next text they read. If all we're doing is asking questions about *Winn-Dixie*, readers will probably have a solid understanding of that book by the last page—certainly an important goal. But those questions, even the ones I posed, don't inform the study of subsequent books.

How can we ensure that students both reap the requisite knowledge from each text they read and acquire skills to pursue the meaning of other texts independently? I suggest we coach students to ask themselves four basic questions as they reflect on a specific portion of any text, even the shortest:

- What is the author *telling* me here?
- Are there any hard or important *words*?
- What does the author want me to *understand*?

- How does the author play with *language* to add to meaning?

If students take time to ask themselves these questions while reading and become skillful at answering them, there'll be less need for the teacher to do all the asking. For this to happen, we must develop students' capacity to observe and analyze.

Focus on Observing and Analyzing

First things first: See whether students have noticed the details of a passage and can recount those details in their own words. Note that the challenge here isn't to be brief (as in a summary); it's to be accurate, precise, and clear.

The recent focus on finding evidence in a text has sent students (even in primary grades) scurrying back to their books to retrieve a quote that validates their opinion. But to paraphrase what that quote means in a student's own language, rather than the author's, is more difficult than you might think. Try it with any paragraph. Expressing the same meaning with different words often requires going back to that text a few times to get the details just right.

Paraphrasing is pretty low on Bloom's continuum of lower- to higher-order thinking, yet many students stumble even here. This is the first stop along the journey to close reading. If students can't paraphrase the basic content of a passage, how can they dig for its deeper meaning? The second basic question about hard or important words encourages students to zoom in on precise meaning.

When students are satisfied that they have a basic grasp of what the author is telling them, they're ready to move on to analyzing the fine points of content. If students begin their analysis by asking themselves the third question—What does the author want me to understand in this passage?—they'll be on their way to making appropriate inferences, determining what the author is trying to show without stating it directly. We might encourage students to ask themselves questions like these:

- Who is speaking in the passage?
- Who seems to be the main audience? (To whom is the narrator speaking?)
- What is the first thing that jumps out at me? Why?
- What's the next thing I notice? Are these two things connected? How? Do they seem to be saying *different* things?
- What seems important here? Why?
- What does the author mean by _____? What exact words lead me to this meaning?
- Is the author trying to convince me of something? What? How do I know?
- Is there something missing from this passage that I expected to find? Why might the author have left this out?
- Is there anything that could have been explained more thoroughly for greater clarity?
- Is there a message or main idea? What in the text led me to this conclusion?
- How does this sentence/passage fit into the text as a whole?

Students who learn to ask themselves such questions are reading with the discerning eye of a careful reader. We can also teach students to read carefully with the eye of a writer, which means helping them analyze craft.

How a text is written is as important as the content itself in getting the author's message across. Just as a movie director focuses the camera on a particular detail to get you to view the scene the way he or she wants you to, authors play with words to get you to see a text *their* way. Introducing students to some of the tricks authors use opens students' minds to an entirely new realm in close reading.

Figure 9.1 provides a list of craft techniques to which we might introduce students to encourage close reading, along with questions that might help students explore how an author uses each craft in a text.

Figure 9.1: Craft Techniques and Related Questions for Close Reading

Craft Technique	Possible Questions
Imagery, including comparisons: • Similes • Metaphors • Personification • Figurative language • Symbols	What is being compared? Why is the comparison effective? (typically because of the clear, strong, or unusual connection between the two) What symbols are present? Why did the author choose these symbols?
Word choice	What word(s) stand out? Why? (typically vivid words, unusual choices, or a contrast to what a reader expects) How do particular words get us to look at characters or events in a particular way? Do they evoke an emotion? Did the author use nonstandard English or words in another language? Why? What is the effect? Are there any words that could have more than one meaning? Why might the author have played with language in this way?
Tone and voice	What *one* word describes the tone? Is the voice formal or informal? If it seems informal, how did the author make it that way? If it's formal, what makes it formal? Does the voice seem appropriate for the content?
• Sentence structure • Short sentence • Long sentences • Sentence fragments • Sentences in which word order is important • Questions	What stands out about the way this sentence is written? Why did the author choose a short sentence here? (for example, so it stands out from sentences around it, for emphasis) Why did the author make this sentence really long? (for example, to convey the "on and on" sense of the experience) Why did the author write a fragment here? (for example, for emphasis or to show a character's thoughts) Based on the order of the words in this sentence, which word do you think is the most important? Why? What was the author trying to show by placing a particular word in a certain place?

Getting students to ask themselves the four general questions and the more specific questions about content and craft is a long-term goal. If we want to create close readers who are also independent readers, we need to explicitly teach how to approach a text to uncover its multiple layers of meaning. In the meantime, we'll need to come to class prepared to ask important text-dependent questions when students' own questioning fails to produce a deep understanding. But those questions need to be more than "text-dependent"; they need to represent the full range of the Common Core standards.

College and career readiness begins in the primary grades. With the right tools, we can build close reading skills even with our youngest readers.

References

Coleman, D., & Pimentel, S. (2012). *Revised publishers' criteria for the Common Core State Standards in English Language Arts and Literacy, grades 3–12.* Retrieved from Student Achievement Partners at www.achievethecore.org/stealthesetools

National Assessment Governing Board. (2002). *Reading Framework for the 2003 National Assessment of Educational Progress (Appendix A).* Washington, DC: Author.

Partnership for Assessment of Readiness for College and Careers. (2011). *PARCC model content frameworks: English language arts/literacy grades 3–11.* Retrieved from www.parcconline.org/sites/parcc/files/PARCCMCFELALiteracyAugust2012_FINAL.pdf

Paul, R., & Elder, L. (2008). *How to read a paragraph: The art of close reading.* Dillon Beach, CA: Foundation for Critical Thinking Press.

Student Achievement Partners. (2012). *Close reading exemplar: Grade 3, "Because of Winn-Dixie."* Retrieved from Student Achievement Partners.

Nancy Boyles (nancyboyles@comcast.ne) is the graduate reading program coordinator for Southern Connecticut State University in New Haven and author of six books, including *That's a GREAT Answer! Teaching Literature-Response Strategies to Elementary, ELL, and Struggling Readers* (Maupin House Publishing, 2011).

Originally published in the December 2012/January 2013 issue of *Educational Leadership*, *70*(4): pp. 36–41.

10

The Challenge of Challenging Text

Timothy Shanahan, Douglas Fisher, and Nancy Frey

When teachers understand what makes texts complex, they can better support their students in reading them.

How is reading complex text like lifting weights? Just as it's impossible to build muscle without weight or resistance, it's impossible to build robust reading skills without reading challenging text. The common core state standards in language arts treat text difficulty as akin to weight or resistance in an exercise program.

This is in contrast to most past discussion of this topic, which emphasized how overly complex text may impede learning. Such discussion therefore focused on developing various readability schemes and text gradients to help teachers determine which books might be too hard for their students. The new standards instead propose that teachers move students purposefully through increasingly complex text to build skill and stamina.

What Makes Text Complex?

To help students learn to read complex texts, teachers need to answer the question, What do we mean when we say that a text is difficult?

Readability formulas usually answer this question by measuring two factors: challenging vocabulary and long, complex sentences. Here we look at these factors along with several others that also affect readers' ability to comprehend text.

Vocabulary

If you ask students what makes reading hard, they blame the words. And they're right to place so much importance on vocabulary: Authors introduce their ideas through words and phrases, and if readers don't know what these mean, there's little chance that they will make sense of the text. Studies show that higher-order thinking in reading depends heavily on knowledge of word meanings.[1]

Often, textbooks and teachers focus their attention on teaching students the vocabulary words that describe central concepts in science, history, mathematics, or literature. Domain-specific terms, such as *erosion, Newton's third law of motion, rhombus,* and *metaphor,* are sure to receive instructional emphasis in today's classrooms. However, these words are usually surrounded by other essential but more general academic terms, such as *exerts, estimates, determines, distributed, resulting, culminates,* and *classify.* These words, every bit as much as those in the first list, are used in particular ways in the various disciplines and warrant instructional attention. Students' ability to comprehend a piece of text depends on the number of unfamiliar domain-specific words and new general academic terms they encounter.

Sentence Structure

Words are not the whole picture. Sentence structure matters, too, because it determines how the words operate together. Thus, understanding the sentence *"The stork was walking in the beautiful cornfield"* requires more than just being able to define individual words. The sentence must also tell the reader how the ideas expressed by these words fit together (Which stork? Where was the stork? What was it doing?). If the text instead said, "*Stork beautiful the walking in was the cornfield,*" all the same ideas would have been presented, yet readers would not understand the meaning.

Other aspects of sentence structure can determine how hard it is for readers to make sense of text. Shorter sentences, for example, tend to be easier to read than longer sentences; presumably, they put less demand on the reader's working memory. Longer sentences are likely to include multiple phrases or clauses, so they tend to include more ideas that have to be related to one another. They also have a greater density (longer noun or verb phrases) and more embedding (more complex relationships).

Authors construct such complicated sentences for a variety of reasons. In some cases, complex sentence structures are necessary to communicate the complexity of the information itself—thus the long noun phrases common in science. In literary passages, long-sentence writers like William Faulkner or Evelyn Waugh may be trying to get readers to slow down and explore the architecture of the thoughts and feelings being expressed. In attempting to convey emotional complexity, we might write a sentence like this:

> The yellow snow blower that my father bought for my mother for their 15th wedding anniversary last year is now sitting in the garage, under a pile of old boxes and newspapers, where she left it that night, just before she threw her mobile phone, the one with my picture on it, at dad, and burst into tears.

The many layered phrases in this sentence express the complicated emotions connected with the events better than a series of shorter, clearer sentences would do. However, such sentences can be hard to untangle because of the demands they place on working memory: What happened just before the mother threw her phone? Who burst into tears? The verb phrase is so deeply embedded in this sentence that it can be hard, at first, to identify what is happening. If students are to interpret the meanings such complex sentence structures convey, they need to learn how to make sense of the conventions of text—phrasing, word order, punctuation, and language.

Coherence

Another challenge concerns how particular words, ideas, and sentences in text connect with one another, a feature referred to as *coherence*. Authors use pronouns, synonyms, ellipses, and other tools to connect the ideas across text. For example, take this simple passage:

> John and Mary went to space camp. They liked it there. Of course, boys often like rockets, but Mary, too, enjoyed it.

The first sentence tells about something two children did. To make sense of the second sentence, the reader has to recognize that the pronoun *they* refers to the two children who were named in the first sentence and that *there* refers to *space camp*. Similarly, to interpret the third sentence, the reader has to link *boys* to *John* and recognize that *it* means the same thing as *there* did in the second sentence.

Younger students often have difficulty making such connections, especially if the ideas are far apart or the referents don't get restated frequently. Distant or complex cohesive links can also be challenging for second-language learners or for older students reading about an unfamiliar topic.

Organization

Ideas can be arranged across text in many ways, some more straightforward than others. For example, some kinds of text—such as a science experiment or a recipe—order events in a time sequence. This would also be true of some fiction or historical stories, but not all of them. You will most likely never see a writer play around with a time sequence in presenting a science experiment, but flashbacks in literature and non-sequential presentations of events in historical writing are common and important.

Other organizational structures include compare-contrast and problem-solution. For example, in science texts, detailed comparisons between species like alligators and crocodiles or between concepts like meiosis and mitosis are common. Similarly, problem-solution structures are evident in both science and social studies; for example, an essay might explain multiple causes of water pollution and then explore multiple solutions for each of these causes. Some organizational structures are used to organize particular text features; for example, a social studies textbook may include particular categories of detailed information (history, geography, economics, and culture) in each chapter.

Students who are aware of the patterns authors use to communicate complex information have an advantage in making sense of text. For example, it's easier to follow *Moby Dick* if you know that it is a narrative of a voyage punctuated by a series of digressions—that one chapter might move the story forward, followed by another that describes the anatomy of whales, the history of whaling, or a sermon that one might hear in a whaling-town church in the 19th century.

Background Knowledge

Vocabulary, sentence structure, coherence, and organization can all be determined by closely analyzing the text itself. A final determinant of text difficulty, however, depends on the reader's prior knowledge.

For example, Ernest Hemingway's *The Old Man and the Sea* is often recommended for use with adolescents. Hemingway's language is spare and plain; he uses common words, and his sentences are often short, without embedding or complexity. A text gradient analysis would place this text at a 6th grade reading level.

Yet many students at this age would have difficulty understanding this beautiful book. The reason is obviously not in the book itself but in the interaction between the reader and the book. Few preteens have had the emotional experiences that would prepare them to understand the old man's determination to maintain hope and dignity in the face of overwhelming odds. Students' background knowledge, including developmental, experiential, and cognitive factors, influences their ability to understand the explicit and inferential qualities of a text.

What Can Teachers Do About Text Complexity?

Knowledge of text complexity can help teachers design three important components of literacy instruction: building skills, establishing purpose, and fostering motivation.

Build Skills

Let's face it: Some students can't make sense of a complex text because they can't decode it. Any older student who still struggles with decoding needs intervention to address this difficulty.

But even students who have basic decoding skills sometimes struggle to deploy these skills easily and accurately enough to get a purchase on challenging text. To help these students develop reading fluency, teachers should give them lots of practice with reading the same text, as well as instruction to help them develop a stronger sense of where to pause in sentences, how to group words, and how their voices should rise or fall at various junctures when reading aloud.

Fluency instruction becomes more powerful when it's taught not as an end in itself, but rather in the context of students' attempts to make sense of a particular text. True fluency is not merely lining up one sentence after another and reading them aloud quickly; it's also maintaining understanding across a text. Therefore, fluency instruction should emphasize sentence structure and meaning. Teachers should have students pause to discuss the meaning of the text. They should pair repeated readings of the same text with questions that require the student to read closely for detail and key ideas.

Ongoing, solid vocabulary instruction is another essential component to help students develop skill in reading complex text. This instruction should focus not just on domain-specific words and phrases that describe the central concepts in the subject area, but also on general academic words. Effective vocabulary instruction usually provides a rich exploration of word meanings, in which students do more than just copy dictionary definitions—they consider synonyms, antonyms, categories, and specific examples for the words under study.

Students also explore the connections among words, considering other words in the same category, comparing and contrasting words with similar meanings, evaluating or constructing analogies, and building word webs. They also have opportunities to use the words in reading, writing, speaking, listening, drawing, and even physically acting them out. As students analyze the use of the vocabulary terms in text, teachers can guide them to think about the meanings that the authors intended to convey (for example, the differences in implication between *nosey* and *curious*, or *cheap* and *frugal*).

Establish Purpose

Recently, we were asked to explain why a passage about deserts was challenging for readers. As we started to read the text, we noticed its beautiful language, vivid imagery, and well-wrought descriptions. Despite its beauty, however, we found it hard to make sense of this passage. The problem was that we couldn't tell whether it was meant to be a literary text or a scientific one. Without knowing what kind of text we were reading or what we were expected to do with the information, we had no idea what to attend to.

Students often find themselves in this kind of bind. Younger children frequently encounter hybrid texts that combine a narrative story with expository information. For example, in the Magic School Bus books, the characters take field trips to learn about electricity, weather, dinosaurs, and other topics. When reading these books, children need to determine whether to focus on the story of the field trip or the information about the concepts. Until they figure it out, they may feel confused.

Older students are confronted with texts from science, history, mathematics, and literature; and they have to grasp the purposes for reading each of these texts so that they can focus their attention appropriately. For example, science texts focus heavily on causation. These texts convey information about what causes what, but they are not typically concerned with the intention behind these events. Students reading a science text may learn that apples grow on trees and that birds eat them, which plays an important role in spreading the seeds around, which creates even more apple trees; however, readers will not be expected to question whether apples grow on trees intentionally so that birds may eat them. In contrast, in reading history and literature, readers need to be concerned with not just the causes of events, but also the human intentions behind these causes.

In clearly communicating the purpose of reading to students, teachers should not convey so much information that it spoils the reading or enables students to participate in class without completing the reading; rather, they should let students know what learning to expect from the reading. For the text about deserts, for example, establishing the purpose, "Determine the difference between desert and tundra biomes" would direct the reading differently from establishing the purpose, "Examine the author's use of imagery and consider how you could apply it in your own writing." Although both of these purposes are worthwhile, reading for one purpose while performing a task for another would likely result in confusion and even failure. When students struggle to understand the task, they pay less attention to the text itself.

Over time, as students read with purpose, they develop background knowledge and a deeper understanding of the organizational structures authors use to convey information. This understanding gives students access to increasingly complex texts.

Foster Motivation and Persistence

Learning to read challenging text is similar to undergoing physical therapy. Initially, such therapy is often painful and exhausting, and it's tempting to cheat on the exercises a bit. Physical therapists have to focus not only on the muscle groups that need to be strengthened or stretched, but also on the patient's motivation. They need to keep the patient's head in the game, because working past the pain is beneficial.

Similarly, it can be tough for students to hang in there and stick with a text that they have to labor through, looking up words, puzzling over sentences, straining to make connections. Teachers may be tempted to try to make it easier for students by avoiding difficult texts. The problem is, easier work is less likely to make readers stronger. Teachers need to motivate students to keep trying, especially when the level of work is increasing. The payoff comes from staying on track.

A good physical therapist knows what good teachers know: You need to create successive successes. Students experience success in the company of their teacher, who combines complex texts with effective instruction. They apply their growing competence outside the company of their teacher by reading texts that match their independent reading ability. Over time, they engage in close reading of texts of their own choosing, as well as assigned texts that build their subject-area knowledge. All the while, they set goals with their teachers so that they can gauge their own progress. Forward motion toward a goal matters.

No More Guesswork

Gone are the days when text was judged as difficult solely on the basis of sentence length and syllable count. We now know that many factors affect text complexity. With this increased understanding, teachers do not have to rely on intuition to figure out which books their students can handle. Instead, teachers can select texts worthy of instruction and align their instructional efforts to ensure that all their students read complex, interesting, and important texts.

Endnote

[1]Stahl, S. A., & Fairbanks, M. M. (1986). The effects of vocabulary instruction: A model-based meta-analysis. *Review of Educational Research, 56,* 72–110.

Timothy Shanahan (shanahan@uic.edu) is a professor and department chair, Department of Curriculum and Instruction, University of Illinois, Chicago. **Douglas Fisher** (dfisher@mail.sdsu.edu) and **Nancy Frey** (nfrey@mail.sdsu.edu) are professors in the Department of Teacher Education at San Diego State University, California.

Originally published in the March 2012 issue of *Educational Leadership, 69*(6): pp. 58–62.

Reading Through a Disciplinary Lens

Connie Juel, Heather Hebard, Julie Park Haubner, and Meredith Moran

Understanding how to think like a scientist, writer, or historian can provide students with new insights as they tackle a text.

Young faces are turned toward 8-year-old Elena. Their eyes are alert; they're waiting to hear what she has to say. Someone has just asked her why she really likes the book *One Tiny Turtle* (Candlewick, 2001) by Nicola Davies. Elena turns to page 6 and says, "Listen," as she reads the first sentence. "Far, far out to sea, land is only a memory, and empty sky touches the water." Her teacher, Ms. Ancova, can feel the magic of the sentence as Elena reads it.

Both Elena and Ms. Ancova anticipate the next question a student asks: "Why did you like that sentence?"

"I can see it in my mind," Elena replies, "the sky touching the water, and then, 'land is only a memory.' That really makes us understand how long it's been since that turtle has been on land."

Ms. Ancova is delighted that Elena is both visualizing images and appreciating writer craft. She makes a note to add a discussion of figurative language to her writing craft lessons and then goes back to listening to her students.

"I agree with you, Elena," states Jacob. "I like how the author makes us see the turtle's size. When the turtle is a baby, she says it's 'not much bigger than a bottle top.' And then when the turtle is about two, she says it's 'bigger than a dinner plate.'"

"And then," adds Kiah, "on page 21, when the turtle is over 30, the author says, 'She's big as a barrel now.'"

Thinking Like a Scientist

"Do turtles get bigger than a barrel? How long do they live, anyway?" wonders Marcos.

"I want to know that, too," Elena adds. "And I wonder how we know that a turtle grows up and returns to lay its eggs on the *exact same* beach where it was born. I mean, was someone there on the beach when a baby turtle came out of the egg and then somehow followed the turtle for years in the sea?"

Not only is Elena looking at text through a literary lens, but she is also bringing a scientific eye to it. Ms. Ancova always seems to be short on time to devote to science and social science in her 3rd grade class, so when a text appears during language arts time that can serve as a springboard to scientific or historical investigation, she seizes on that link. She says, "You know, both Marcos and Elena have a scientific inquiry. Marcos wonders how long loggerhead turtles live, and Elena wonders how we actually know that loggerheads return to the *exact same* beach where they were born to deposit their eggs. Both Elena and Marcos have turned their wondering into a scientific question."

"How will you go about answering your questions, Marcos and Elena?" queries Ms. Ancova.

"Well," says Elena. "I think I'm going to start by going to *National Geographic*'s Web site. ..."

In her research, Elena will discover that there is some doubt whether all loggerheads undertake this round-trip swim. She will be fascinated to learn that scientists track turtles by putting a beeping radio transmitter on their shells, which enables them to track the turtles by satellite. She may wonder whether they do this with other animals—and that will lead to new questions. She may wonder, too, whether the beeping is loud and bothers the turtles. She may imagine different tracking devices, maybe ones that she will invent someday.

Why a Disciplinary Lens?

Elena views text through disciplinary lenses. Such specific focusing and refocusing gives a depth to comprehension that more generic comprehension strategies may not provide. Although Elena can apply commonly taught strategies like visualization, prediction, or summarization, her deep engagement with the text comes from the disciplinary focuses of thinking like a scientist and thinking like a writer.

Much like a photographer changing lenses on a camera, Elena can home in on a specific literary device or question an author about his or her scientific evidence. Like the photographer, however, Elena—like all readers—can only focus well on one thing at a time. Ms. Ancova knows this, too, so she will often tell her students which lens they might consider for a specific text. When a text lends itself to a disciplinary view that they have discussed in class, she will encourage students to listen to or read the text with that focus in mind.

Before the class read *One Tiny Turtle*, Ms. Ancova explained that they were going to read a text written by a writer who uses lots of great images and that because the author is a zoologist, she includes scientific statements in her books as well. Ms. Ancova encouraged her students to think alternately like a scientist and like a writer as they read this book.

Viewing a text from a disciplinary perspective does not compensate for lack of vocabulary or conceptual knowledge that can quickly deter comprehension. It does, however, give the reader an idea of how to proceed when there is a roadblock. This is one reason that taking a disciplinary stance is recommended for teachers working with English language learners (Brock, Lapp, Salas, & Townsend, 2009).

Take Jenny, a 2nd grader, who could decode text considerably above grade level but whose reading comprehension was limited by her oral vocabulary (Juel, 1994). Jenny was interested in reading about rocks. Yet she was stymied when she encountered statements like, "There are various minerals in granite." She acknowledged, with considerable frustration, "I don't know much about rocks. I wouldn't know granite if I sat on it."

Jenny might not be so defeated if she had a way of thinking through this scientific subject matter. If she knew that observation might help her, she might seek out a photograph of granite or, better yet, find a rock sample. She might stare at a piece of granite and notice in it the shiny reflections of bits of translucent quartz, the flakes of black mica, and the creamy pink specks of feldspar. Even if she could not name these minerals, she could see how granite was composed of them. She might then wonder why these minerals adhere to one another. What force in nature could twist and hold them together? What force creates that glasslike quartz? Wonder, question, observe, think, question…

There are two crucial reasons to include disciplinary frames in our instruction. One relates to reading comprehension: Disciplinary habits of mind can extend students' reading comprehension by providing scaffolds for thinking. If a student knows that studying the natural world entails careful observation and thinking, then the student is more likely to observe and think about what he or she sees or to wonder about the causes of particular phenomena.

If a student knows that scientific claims involve careful collection of evidence, he or she is more likely to ask for evidence from those who make scientific claims rather than accept those claims at face value. Indeed, students who question and challenge one another for evidence in their text discussions typically acquire the habit of asking questions as well as the expectation that they will continually learn new things (Resnick & Nelson-LeGall, 1996). Of course, what counts as evidence depends on the discipline. In providing literary evidence, it is acceptable to say how words make you feel. But in science, feeling will not get you far.

The second reason to support a disciplinary stance is because of technology. No longer do students jump to a set of printed encyclopedias; rather, they jump on the Internet. To understand how to evaluate all the information that is readily available online, students need to know the standard for evidence in a given arena. How, for example, will a student judge whether an Internet entry about loggerhead turtles reflects someone's desire to save a given stretch of coastline (as admirable as that motive might be) or is based on scientific evidence? Understanding how to think like a scientist, to think like a writer, and to think like a historian can provide students with direction as they read particular texts.

Thinking Like a Writer

In Mr. Salazar's 2nd grade classroom, the students have been studying narrative in their reading and writing. Today, as they think about how authors write their leads—their opening sentences— Mr. Salazar and his students revisit a read-aloud book, *Too Many Tamales* (Putnam, 1996), by Gary Soto. The class has already taken time to delight in the rich illustrations, feel the suspense of the dramatic plot, and respond to the texts as readers. Now the class rereads the lead, which Salazar has written on chart paper: "Snow drifted through the streets, and now that it was dusk, Christmas trees glittered in the windows." Students talk in pairs about what they notice and then share their comments with their classmates:

"You can tell what time of year it is and where you are," says Cerise.

"Yeah," says Robert, "it tells the setting."

"But it doesn't just say 'It was Christmas,'" adds Maya. "You can see the place because he describes what it looks like."

The class reads the excerpt again, and students point out the descriptive language, such as the snow *drifted* and the trees *glittered*. Mr. Salazar then helps students connect their observations to the writer's purpose. "Why might Gary Soto have begun his book with this description?" Mr. Salazar wants his students to understand that writers make composing decisions all the time—and that they do this with their audience and their purpose in mind.

The students decide that beginning a story with a description of a setting helps readers know where the story takes place and enables them to imagine the scene. Next, Mr. Salazar asks the students to give this type of lead a name—they decide to call it a "descriptive setting lead." He knows that building a shared vocabulary for discussing craft will help his students talk about and use crafting techniques (Pritchard & Honeycutt, 2007). He also understands that although getting students to notice craft is a good start, he will need to provide more instruction to help these young writers use the techniques they notice (Hillocks, 1987).

In subsequent lessons, he will provide opportunities for students to try this kind of lead for their own purposes and audiences. He might organize inquiry activities to help students think about describing scenes using sensory detail (Smith & Hillocks, 1989). He might model the strategy of visualization to develop setting, thinking aloud as he visualizes the scene of a narrative he is writing. Or he might teach a technique, showing how he revises his lead to use vivid verbs, as Soto does (Graham, 2006).

As Mr. Salazar's class continues its study of narrative, the students will notice all kinds of things about texts. They will talk about the foreshadowing in the lead of Anthony Browne's *Piggybook* (Dragonfly Books, 1990); the short, suspenseful sentences in Donald Crews's *Shortcut* (Greenwillow Books, 1996); and the simile in Jane Yolen's *Owl Moon* (Philomel, 1987). They will map out the structures of the narratives they read and notice how characters often change through the events in the plot. And they will begin to notice the craft they study in other books they read.

Thinking like writers can support reading comprehension in a several ways. Students become more attuned to writing craft—craft that is closely tied to the meaning of the text. For example, students who have studied foreshadowing are more apt to notice it in their own reading and can use it to support their predictions. Moreover, when students learn how to read closely, they learn a whole new way to talk about and appreciate texts. They see the value of lingering with a text, rereading to appreciate its literary qualities.

Thinking like a writer also supports the development of critical literacy. Frequent discussions that speculate about the author's purpose and audience help students realize the intentionality behind the texts they read. For example, a 6th grade class might read and write feature articles. They might discover that authors of these articles frame their topics in persuasive ways. They might also learn some techniques of persuasion, such as the strategic use of an emotionally appealing anecdote or alarming statistics.

Young readers who are aware of such strategies are better equipped to critique the texts they encounter. As our students move into adolescence and adulthood, they are exposed to more and more texts that aim to persuade them to buy, vote, or think in a particular way. Thinking like a writer can help students critically navigate these texts.

Thinking Like a Historian

We often associate history with memorizing important dates in singsong rhymes, doing a project on a famous American, or enacting a fun simulation of Colonial days. But learning history can also be an opportunity to practice reading behaviors that can transfer into real-world situations.

Stacie, a 7th grade language arts teacher who teaches a class period of history, is dismayed by the textbook's dry treatment of the U.S. Constitution. She wants her students to appreciate the importance and relevance of this document. So she finds stories of students denied their First Amendment rights and teaches a successful unit. Her students are emotionally invested in the tales of children who were affected directly by the Constitution.

Stacie values her students' personal responses and helps them relate their experiences to the texts, but she struggles with connecting her strengths in teaching reading to the discipline of history. What is new for Stacie, and for most of us who still think of history as learning about what happened in the past, is an understanding that the practice of history is a profoundly literate activity that has an important place in the school curriculum.

History is distinctive among the disciplines in seeking out many sources of information and wrestling with their contradictions and problems to tell a compelling narrative about a human event. Historians are experts at synthesizing huge amounts of texts. But how can the complex reading behaviors of a professional historian help improve a 7th grader's understanding of the world?

First, historians rarely learn from textbooks. We must acknowledge the limitations of the textbooks and nonfiction trade books that are the bulk of our school texts. The reality is that teachers can no longer control the amount or quality of information that students encounter. As Wineburg and Martin (2004) so vividly claim, "Ask any middle schooler with a research project how to spell the word *library*, and you'll get a six-letter response: G-O-O-G-L-E" (p. 43). And herein lies the danger. When a student searches for information on how Barack Obama got elected, for example, many of the Web sites listed contain varying degrees of bias and error. None of them even attempts to answer the question of how such a historic event happened. How can we even begin to help students decipher these results?

We can teach students that texts that deal with historical events often have real authors—as opposed to the faceless authors of textbooks, whose chief purpose is to write engaging, informative, and coherent text. Real authors have motivations for writing, and those motivations affect the credibility of their words. Consideration of the author's perspective, in historians' language, is called *sourcing*.

Sourcing is the first and most instinctive reading move that historians make—and that students often *don't* make (Wineburg, 1991).

In this information age, students cannot wait until they are adults to acquire this skill. We can begin this conversation by providing even young students with texts that have a point of view and a visible author. Understanding who the author is and why he or she is taking this point of view is just as important as understanding what the author is saying.

In the instance of the student who searches online for information about how Barack Obama got elected, the historically minded student would make a point of noticing that one of the first Web sites retrieved—"Witness the death of journalism!" it exclaims—is authored by a filmmaker selling an inflammatory documentary about "media malpractice." When reading a textbook passage about the causes of the American Revolution or conflicting editorials about whether the United States should continue to fight in Afghanistan, the historically trained young reader would know that rarely are such complex events a simple story of good versus evil or right versus wrong. This reader would actively seek out more information to attain a more nuanced understanding.

It may be messy, long, and difficult, but the act of sifting through puzzling, conflicting, and biased texts should constitute at least part of a student's experience. This is the everyday work of the historian.

Of course, historians—like all good readers—also predict, reread, self-monitor, and so forth. But a distinctive trait of the discipline is the ability to synthesize vast amounts of text into a cohesive narrative, which is precisely the kind of critical thinking that we want our students to do. Historians are experts at corroborating information across different kinds of texts and perspectives. From them, we can learn how to help students think flexibly about multiple sources of information.

Start Young

We should cast a disciplinary lens over most texts—even when we're reading these texts with young children. Consider how a kindergarten teacher planted the seed for scientific reasoning, including the process of looking at data and forming hypotheses, while her students were reading the predictable text in Amy Casey's little book, *Can You Find It?* (Modern Curriculum Press, 1997).

On each page is a colored photo that shows an animal camouflaged in its natural surroundings. Underneath each photo appears the text, "Can you find the _____?" with the appropriate animal's name included (cat, frog, fox, and so forth). A striped house cat blends into the light and dark patterns of the foliage around it; a green frog perches on a green leaf; a white Arctic fox stands on snow. The teacher asks her students, "Why do you think the fox is white? Why do you think the frog is green? Why is the cat brown with black stripes? What is the big idea here?"

As a teacher, how might you decide which lens to adopt for a text? Take into account the message in the text and the vocabulary load. Think about what students might discuss. Clarify the discipline involved and the thinking specific to that discipline. Give students the opportunity to look at texts through the three useful lenses of science, writing, and history.

References

Brock, C., Lapp, D., Salas, R., & Townsend, D. (2009). *Academic literacy for English learners*. New York: Teachers College Press.

Graham, S. (2006). Strategy instruction and the teaching of writing: A meta-analysis. In C. A. MacArthur, S. Graham, & J. Fitzgerald (Eds.), *Handbook of writing research* (pp. 187–207). New York: Guilford.

Hillocks, G., Jr. (1987). Synthesis of research on teaching writing. *Educational Leadership, 44*(8), 71–82.

Juel, C. (1994). *Learning to read and write in one elementary school*. New York: Springer-Verlag.

Pritchard, R. J., & Honeycutt, R. L. (2007). Best practices in implementing a process approach to teaching writing. In S. Graham, C. A. MacArthur, & J. Fitzgerald (Eds.), *Best practices in writing instruction* (pp. 28–49). New York: Guilford.

Resnick, L., & Nelson-LeGall, S. (1996). Socializing intelligence. In L. Smith, J. Dockrell, & P. Tomlinson (Eds.), *Piaget, Vygotsky, and beyond* (pp. 145–158). London: Routledge.

Smith, M. W., & Hillocks, G., Jr. (1989). What inquiring writers need to know. *English Journal, 78*(2), 58–63.

Wineburg, S. S. (1991). Historical problem solving: A study of the cognitive processes used in the evaluation of documentary and pictorial evidence. *Journal of Educational Psychology, 83*(1), 73–87.

Wineburg, S., & Martin, D. (2004). Reading and rewriting history. *Educational Leadership, 62*(1), 42–45.

Connie Juel (cjuel@stanford.edu) is Professor of Education and **Heather Hebard** (hhebard@stanford.edu), **Julie Park Haubner** (haubner@stanford.edu), and **Meredith Moran** (mmoran@stanford.edu) are doctoral candidates at Stanford University, Stanford, California.

Originally published in the March 2010 issue of *Educational Leadership, 67*(6): pp. 12–17.

The Power of Purposeful Reading

Cris Tovani

To help students master challenging text, teachers must clarify the meaning behind the mission.

Students often seem mystified when asked to determine what is important in an assigned reading. Teachers see this confusion when students' book pages are overly highlighted in bright yellow. Media specialists see it in requests for printing out massive numbers of documents from the Internet. Parents see it when their children complete reading assignments and equate note taking with copying entire chapters. It's frustrating for everyone concerned, but especially for the students. As one of my 11th grade students told me,

> Most of the time, I don't like to be told what to think, but at school I have to be told, especially when I read hard stuff. I have no idea what's important.

At the beginning of the year, I ask my students how they know something is important in an assigned reading. More often than not, they reply, "Anything in bold print is important." When I ask why bold print makes text important, they respond, "I don't know why. It just does."

Clearly, these students are using ineffective reading strategies that seem logical to them. As Mike Rose notes,

> Every day in our schools and colleges young people face reading and writing tasks that seem hard or unusual, that confuse them, that they fail. But if you can get close enough to their failure, you'll find knowledge that the assignment didn't tap, ineffective rules and strategies that have logic of their own.[1]

Several years ago, I surveyed my fellow teachers at Smoky Hill High School in Colorado to find out what skill they thought students most needed to improve their comprehension of assigned readings. The number one response was that students don't know how to determine what is important in the text.

I agree with my colleagues. Being able to distinguish big ideas from minutiae is a skill that adolescent readers desperately need. But how do we teach it?

Reflecting on My Own Reading

I can often inform my teaching practice by carefully observing my own processes as a reader, noticing what I do when I start to struggle with a text and drawing on my own thinking strategies. The same strategies that I use to help myself are often useful to students.

Recently, I decided to pay attention to how I determine what's important when reading an unfamiliar text, hoping that I would gain insight into how to help my students do the same. I needed to select a text that was unfamiliar to me, preferably with content out of my comfort zone. I chose a chapter in a chemistry book that several of my students were reading—and complaining about.

As I started to read the chapter on ionic and covalent bonds, my mind began to wander. When I forced my attention back to the text, consciously watching my thinking, I realized that I was in trouble. I had no way of determining importance. My two stumbling blocks were lack of background knowledge and lack of clarity about how I would use the information. Because my background knowledge in this topic was limited, I thought everything was important. Because I didn't know how the information was going to be used, I decided to try to remember everything in bold print. I quickly discovered that there was a lot of bold print, and trying to remember the information without directly applying it was nearly impossible.

I concluded that the same thing probably happened to my 11th grade students in this chemistry class, and I began to appreciate what these students went through. But I also realized that if I'd started out with a *purpose* for my reading, I would have had a way to sort out which information was important and which was trivial according to that purpose.

We can't expect students to determine what information is important in a text if they don't know how they are going to use the information. Teachers can help students determine importance by sharing with them the purpose for reading a given text. This purpose may be to ask specific questions as they read. It could be a mission to find a specific piece of information or to read the text and form an opinion.

Giving students a purpose for their reading and telling them what's important to look for may feel like "dumbing down" content. Yet when I retrace my own reading process, I find that when I know why I am reading something, I tend to dig in deeper and work harder. When I know what I'm looking for, I read more effectively than when I think everything on the page is equally important.

I know from teaching English that there are many different ways to read a given text, especially fiction. Among many possibilities, I can simply follow the plot; I can notice how the protagonist changes from the beginning of the novel to the end; I can watch for repetition of words and motifs; or I can analyze the author's use of metaphor. Usually, I notice multiple features as I read. But I rarely encounter a text and notice everything on the first read.

I'm good at reading fiction and have lots of experience knowing what to look for. My students, on the other hand, are not so practiced. If I don't provide a purpose for their reading, they may not notice or remember anything, just as I didn't know what to notice in the chemistry text as an inexperienced reader of that subject.

The Need for Clarity

Too many educators seem to expect students to read the teacher's mind. Last summer, as my daughter Carrie was preparing for her first year in a large, prestigious, and potentially intimidating high school, she took advantage of older students' wisdom to get a feel for the school. She asked every older kid she encountered, "What do I need to do to survive my freshman year?" Interestingly enough, she always got the same answer: "Just figure out what the teachers want. Once you do that, you'll be fine."

After hearing this response over and over again, I asked myself why so many kids feel the need to "figure out" what the teacher wants. Why don't teachers clarify what they want? Then I posed this question in terms of my own teaching practice. I began to wonder whether I make *my* students play the role of mind reader, and if so, why. Do I assume that if I told students what is important they wouldn't read or think? That I would be shirking my responsibilities by not making students figure out what's important on their own? Do I reason that no one in the "real world" is going to tell them what's important when they read something, so they'd better start figuring it out now?

Yet in everyday work situations, people frequently ask questions and get clarification about key documents they read on the job. When a supervisor thinks something is important, he or she usually points it out so that employees can benefit from having a focus.

Purpose is an amazing thing. Purpose not only provides a way to sort information, but it also gives the mind a job so that the reader doesn't just read the words while thinking about something unrelated to the text. If we want our students to wrestle with meaning and work hard to comprehend, teachers will have to limit the scope of reading tasks by making purpose explicit.

Purposeful Guidance

Instead of expecting students to guess what's essential, teachers can greatly improve comprehension by explicitly identifying what information students need to glean from a text. For example, when assigning a reading about the period before the U.S. Civil War, with the eventual goal of discussing causes of the war, the teacher could focus students' attention on that goal. It's not enough to tell students, "Here are all the reasons for the Civil War. Now, go read about them tonight." With such broad brush guidance, students would probably just look at the bold text or highlight randomly as they read. It's more powerful to tell students something like, "Tomorrow we are going to work on an activity that will increase your understanding about how the Civil War got started. While reading this assignment, figure out three incidents that contributed to the war. Mark those places with sticky notes, and on each sticky note describe the incident in your own words." Such instructions provide a way to hold students accountable for understanding and retaining crucial information they read.

When guiding students on what to focus on in assigned readings, I try to be realistic. There is no way my students are going to learn everything I know about any subject in one semester. I get the chance to revisit the curriculum and course of study year after year; my students don't. Teachers must decide—and help students focus on—what is essential to take away from any reading.

One of my favorite tools for helping students focus and retain their thinking as they read is a simple sheet that I call a comprehension constructor. It is both a checklist to guide students through the thinking process and a tangible way to make their thinking clear, which helps me evaluate it. The comprehension constructor shown in Figure 12.1

helps students approach a book of nonfiction, prompting them to use questions they care about to drive their reading.

> **Figure 12.1: How to Read Nonfiction with Purpose**
>
> 1. Study the front and back covers and table of contents of the book and skim through the pages. Jot down four questions you have about the topic.
> 2. Decide which parts of the book you will read. As you read, jot on sticky notes information you learn that helps you address your questions. You should have at least eight sticky notes.
> 3. Write down what you have learned about this topic. Include new questions and any new connections you've made about the subject.

Purpose: Fake It to Make It

Another strategy is helping students invent their own motivating purpose. Because reading difficult or unengaging text without any purpose is deadly, it's essential that we teach students what to do when teachers don't give a clear purpose for a particular reading. I have found that students can focus and comprehend better when they set their own purpose for an assigned reading than when they plunge ahead with no purpose at all. I explicitly teach students to set what I call a *fake purpose*. Fake purposes force readers to pick a focus. Among the suggestions I make for creating a fake purpose are

- *Be a selfish reader.* I tell students to ask themselves how what they read is going to affect them personally. When they expect to get something out of a reading, students put more effort into the task. Being a selfish reader may mean asking such self-serving questions as, How could I use this information? How is this information different from what I already know? Could this make my life easier in any way? These questions may sound vain and trivial, but they are a good place to start creating a personal purpose for reading.

- *Reread with a new purpose.* Rereading can be a great fix-up strategy for a student who has come away from a piece frustrated in terms of comprehension. But rereading only helps when the reader reads differently and with a specific purpose. Reading a chapter in the chemistry textbook while thinking about getting a driver's license isn't going to enable the student to construct meaning. Some of my students' favorite purposes for rereading are to formulate a question the teacher can help answer, paraphrase a section, visualize what happened in a section, and look for an answer to a previously asked question.
- *Read to connect.* I encourage students to always connect their reading to information or experiences that they are already familiar with. By making a conscious effort to relate new information to known information, students can better relate to the topic and more easily retain the information.

The goal of having students set fake purposes is to give them practice in approaching and setting goals for specific kinds of reading. With practice, students become accustomed to looking for and paying attention to certain features in certain texts. For example, after reading many novels, I know to pay attention early on to details of character because character often drives plot.

Readers wield a great deal of power when they learn how to harness purpose. To help students do so, teachers need to strike a balance between spelling out why and how to read a text and helping students find their own motivations. As educators, we have a responsibility to be clear about our instructional purposes. After all, we are the experts of our content.

But it's also important to teach students how to set their own reading purpose when one isn't given. So when students encounter a loan officer or a college professor who wants to play "Guess what you need to know," they will be a step ahead of the game.

Endnote

[1]Rose, M. (1989). *Lives on the boundary* (p. 8). New York: Penguin Books.

Cris Tovani (pete_cris_tovani@msn.com) teaches English at Smoky Hill High School, 16100 E. Smoky Hill Rd., Aurora, CO 80015; 720-886-5643. She is the author of *Do I Really Have to Teach Reading?* (Stenhouse Publishers, 2004).

Originally published in the October 2005 issue of *Educational Leadership*, *63*(2): pp. 48–51.

Opening the Literature Window

Carol Jago

With help from the teacher, students can read books they wouldn't tackle on their own.

I owe a refund to the first 8th graders I taught. Convinced then as I am now that reading was a key to success in school and beyond, I became obsessed with turning reluctant scholars into readers. I made it my mission to find books that I believed would do the work for me, scouring secondhand bookstores and garage sales for anything on skateboarding, surfing, whatever I thought would entice them. I filled my classroom with short, easy-to-read, funny books. Alas, this "build it, and they will come" approach didn't work. Students glanced at the books and told me in no uncertain terms that they hated reading. The only volumes that attracted any attention were The Guinness Book of World Records and *Name Your Baby*. It made no sense. I loved to read. Why didn't they?

Discouraged but determined, I continued to stock my classroom library with books like *Go Ask Alice; My Darling, My Hamburger;* and *The Outsiders;* but I turned for curricular guidance to the work of Lev Vygotsky (1962). Reading that "the only good kind of instruction is that which marches ahead of development and leads it" (p.104), I realized that I was confusing independent reading with literature study. If students can read a book on their own, it probably isn't the best choice for classroom study. For one thing, teachers run the danger of ruining novels like Suzanne Collins's *The Hunger Games* with talk of foreshadowing and with reading-log assignments. Such books are best when swallowed whole and passed from reader to reader.

Young adult fiction offers mirrors wherein students see their own experiences and emotions reflected. These stories help young readers know they are not the first and won't be the last to feel as they do. Literature study, on the other hand, offers students windows to other worlds, other cultures, other times. It poses intellectual challenges, demanding that students stretch and grow.

In *The Anatomy of Influence*, Harold Bloom (2011) proposes three criteria for choosing works to be read, reread, and taught: aesthetic splendor, cognitive power, and wisdom. These seem to me an obvious improvement over short, easy-to-read, and funny. But literature teachers must do more than simply hand out copies of *Romeo and Juliet* and expect 9th graders to be enthralled by its aesthetic splendor.

The Right Instruction

Making complex works accessible to young readers requires artful instruction. But what does such instruction look like? I have a few ideas.

1. Stop telling students that reading is fun.

Reading can be fun, but constant declarations about it put books in competition with video games and other activities that students find easier and more obviously appealing.

If students groan, "I can't do it. This is too hard" as you distribute copies of a 300-page novel, agree with them that it may be hard, but reassure them that with effort and your help they will be able to do it. Experience has taught teenagers that if they complain loudly for long enough, the teacher will often abandon a difficult text for something shorter, simpler, and more fun. Don't fall for it.

2. Tap students' prior knowledge.

An effective way to introduce the major conflict in Sophocles's *Antigone* is to have students write about a time they stood up to authority—preparing them for the argument between Antigone and her uncle, the king, Creon. On the other hand, it would not be particularly effective to prepare students for Lady Macbeth's "Out, damned spot!" speech in *Macbeth* by asking students to talk with a partner about a time they had a stubborn spot on their hands. Make sure that the prior knowledge students explore is relevant to an important issue in the text.

Deborah Wilchek, a teacher at Rockville High School in Montgomery County, Maryland, begins her unit on Zora Neale Hurston's *Their Eyes Were Watching God* by showing students various covers for the novel and inviting them to analyze them. She asks students to consider the significant features of the cover, the key ideas that the images convey, and the possible audience for the book. Opening lessons like this point the way to the central ideas in the work.

3. Address, don't avoid, academic vocabulary.

Instead of looking for books without difficult vocabulary, complex syntax, or figurative language, teach students how to meet these challenges head on. As Isabel Beck, Margaret McKeown, and Linda Kucan explain in *Creating Robust Vocabulary* (2008), new words should be introduced in a meaningful context, instead of as a list that students study in isolation. Rather than preteaching all the hard words in a chapter, teach a few that are crucial to understanding.

For example, I have found that when I am teaching *Julius Caesar*, it is crucial for my 10th graders to grasp Brutus's motivations. Teaching students the meanings of *stoic*, *gullible*, and *idealist* and then asking them to do a close reading of Act 1, Scene 2 looking for evidence of these traits in Brutus's speech to Cassius helps lay the groundwork for later events in the play and deepens their understanding of the new words they are learning.

4. Teach students how to negotiate complex syntax.

Reading long, complicated sentences is a challenge for everyone, but particularly for students in the habit of skimming and scanning Facebook updates. Teachers need to help students slow the pace of their reading for literature and develop the habit of rereading when a sentence doesn't seem to make sense. Rereading difficult passages doesn't have a cool acronym or fancy graphic organizer, but it is the technique experienced readers employ most often. When was the last time you reached for a K-W-L chart when struggling through a challenging text?

Writers like W. E. B. Du Bois don't use complex syntax in books like *The Souls of Black Folk* to annoy their readers but to express complex ideas. And artful instruction doesn't rewrite difficult passages, casting them into simpler prose for ease of digestion, but rather assists students in parsing each phrase to discover the nuances in Du Bois's message. We can't do the work for students. They must do it for themselves. Selecting important sentences for pairs of students to translate into everyday language can be effective for helping students develop confidence with complex syntax. Telling students what Du Bois is saying only reinforces their belief that such reading is beyond them.

It is not possible to read an Emily Dickinson poem once through and understand its cognitive power and aesthetic splendor. However, no student I have ever met would comply with the instruction to read a poem five times over for homework. Artful teachers trick students into rereading. Elizabeth Nelms (1988) had her seniors read the same poem, Ted Hughes's "Deceptions," for homework from Monday through Friday and keep a log of their emerging observations about the images they found. Nelms explains, "As the days passed, the students' observations of the changing weather began to merge with the poet's images as he sought to capture the elusive nature of spring." She created a reason for students to reread and a framework for them to record the development of their own comprehension. I've used this strategy with success for more than 20 years.

5. Hold students accountable for their reading.

In an ideal world, students are motivated to keep up with the reading in order to participate in our rich classroom conversations. In the real world, we sometimes need to hold their feet to the fire. Even the most diligent students sometimes need the threat of a quiz to remind them to keep up with assigned reading. Unfortunately, quizzes are time-consuming to create, duplicate, and correct.

In addition, students who fall behind depend on online resources like SparkNotes to catch up. Rob Thais, a colleague at Santa Monica High School, devised an efficient way to check that students were doing the reading. He goes to the SparkNotes website, prints out the summary of the chapter assigned for homework, and hands it out when students come to class. He then tells students to write three things that occurred in the chapter that don't appear in this paragraph. This simple ploy achieves two purposes: (1) Students now know you are aware that some of them have turned to SparkNotes, and (2) the quizzes are easy to correct.

In too many schools, teachers have stopped assigning homework reading altogether, principally because students have stopped doing it. This is the path to perdition for literature study. If a teacher reads *Lord of the Flies* aloud to a class of 10th graders, the only person becoming a better reader is the teacher.

I sometimes hear that there aren't enough copies of the books to send home with students. In many one-to-one laptop or e-reader programs, the machines must remain at school. This is educational malpractice. Students need to develop the self-discipline and stamina necessary to read for extended periods of time on their own. How else will they be ready for college? In a College Board study of the class of 2010, 54 percent of students found their college courses more difficult than they expected (Hart Research Associates, 2011). This finding will come as no surprise to English teachers struggling to convince high school seniors to read 20 pages of assigned daily reading.

6. Teach cognitively powerful works.

Sandra Stotsky's (2010) research in *Literary Study in Grades 9, 10, and 11: A National Survey* demonstrates that the literature taught in English classes has decreased in complexity over the past decade. In our effort to make literature study more contemporary and relevant, we have lost much of the rigor. It need not have been the case. Works by Toni Morrison, Maxine Hong Kingston, John Edgar Wideman, Jorge Borges, and James Baldwin have all the cognitive power and aesthetic splendor of Charles Dickens, Robert Louis Stevenson, F. Scott Fitzgerald, and Henry David Thoreau. But because works by Morrison and others of her stature pose the very same textual challenges as the earlier works—difficult vocabulary, complex syntax, figurative language, and length—teachers often choose to teach simpler books.

The common core state standards attempt to remedy this downward trend by providing a list of text exemplars to represent the complexity, quality, and range of works students should be taught at each grade level. Critics decry the list as a *de facto* national reading list, but the Common Core State Standards Initiative (n.d.) states that the choices are meant only as guideposts to help educators select texts at a similar reading level.

One exemplar from the grades 2–3 list is William Steig's *Amos and Boris*. Notice the vocabulary and syntactical challenges this sentence from the story poses:

> One night, in a phosphorescent sea, he marveled at the sight of some whales spouting luminous water; and later, lying on the deck of his boat gazing at the immense, starry sky, the tiny mouse Amos, a little speck of a living thing in the vast living universe, felt thoroughly akin to it all.

If students are reading such wondrous words at 8 years old, imagine what they will be capable of at 18.

Rigor for All

The United States needs a reading renaissance. Students need to stretch beyond what's comfortable to tackle challenging texts. They need to spend time reading material that requires focus and concentration, material that they might not attempt on their own. And they need the support and encouragement of teachers who help them open the literary window onto this new world.

References

Beck, I. L., McKeown, M., Kucan, L. (2008). *Creating robust vocabulary.* New York: Guilford Press.

Bloom, H. (2011). *The anatomy of influence: Literature as a way of life.* New Haven, CT: Yale University Press.

Common Core State Standards Initiative. (n.d.). *Common core state standards for English language arts and literacy in history/social studies, science and technical subjects: Appendix B.* Retrieved from www.corestandards.org/assets/Appendix_B.pdf

Nelms, E. (1988). Two Laureates in April: Lyrics of Wordsworth and Ted Hughes. *English Journal, 77*(4), 23–26.

Hart Research Associates. (2011). *One year out: Findings from a national survey among members of the gruduuliny class of 2010.* Retrieved from the College Board at http://media.collegeboard.com/homeOrg/content/pdf/One_Year_Out_key_findings%20report_final.pdf

Steig, W. (1971). *Amos and Boris.* New York: Farrar, Straus, and Giroux.

Stotsky, S. (2010). *Literary study in grades 9, 10, and 11: A national survey.* Retrieved from the Association of Literary Scholars, Critics, and Writers at www.alscw.org/Forum4.pdf

Vgotsky, L. S. (1962). *Thought and language* (E. Hanfmann & G. Vakar, Eds. and Trans.). Cambridge, MA: MIT Press.

Carol Jago (cjago@caroljago.com) has taught middle and high school in Santa Monica, California, for 32 years. She is past president of the National Council of Teachers of English and author of *With Rigor for All: Helping Students Meet Common Core Standards for Reading Literature* (Heinemann 2011).

Originally published in the March 2012 issue of *Educational Leadership, 69*(6): pp. 40–43.

Reading Moves: What Not to Do

Richard L. Allington

In almost every early elementary classroom, you'll see students reading aloud and answering questions about what they've read. It's time for that to change.

Some instructional moves are so common that almost no one notices them anymore. That's true of two moves I observe teachers using for reading instruction in almost every elementary classroom I visit. Both moves—interrupting students to correct their mistakes during oral reading, and asking students low-level questions after they've finished reading—are widespread, despite the fact that no good evidence has ever supported them as effective. At best, both of these moves are unproductive; at worst, they undermine our children's literacy development.

Move 1. Overusing and Misusing Oral Reading

I've been conducting observational studies of classrooms for four decades, and today I observe more oral reading than ever. The sheer volume of oral reading is disturbing, as is the practice of using oral-reading speed and accuracy to make judgments about reading development. In a classic study, Mosenthal (1977) demonstrated that oral reading and silent reading are different processes; a student's skill in oral reading says little about his or her silent reading proficiency, and vice versa.

According to an evaluation of the federal Reading First program (Gamse, Jacob, Horst, Boulay, & Unlu, 2009), our current fascination with oral reading speed has resulted in students who can read aloud faster and more accurately but whose silent reading comprehension has not improved. Given that independent reading with good comprehension is the ultimate goal of literacy instruction, it's puzzling that oral reading activity is so prevalent.

Creating Two Types of Readers

If teachers must continue to use so much oral reading, they should at least reduce its harm by suppressing their tendency to interrupt readers to correct every mistake. The effects of this widespread practice are especially pernicious for struggling readers.

Over 30 years ago, I conducted two observational studies in elementary classrooms, which not only found that oral reading was prevalent, but also that it was used differently with good and with poor readers (Allington, 1980, 1984). One difference was the amount of oral-reading practice that students experienced. Good readers were more likely to read silently during their reading lessons than were struggling readers. Because most people can read much faster silently than they can read aloud, the result was that struggling readers read fewer than half as many words daily as good readers did. This deficit in sheer reading volume is exactly the opposite of what lagging readers need (Torgeson & Hudson, 2006).

Even more troubling than the simple loss of reading practice, though, was the tendency for classroom teachers to interrupt struggling readers both more often and differently than they interrupted good readers. Teachers typically interrupted struggling readers immediately, even before the student had pronounced the whole word that was causing difficulty. In contrast, teachers waited longer before interrupting good readers, usually until the end of the sentence or even the end of the page.

These differences in the timing of interruptions may explain another observation: Teachers tended to correct struggling readers by focusing on surface-level features while encouraging good readers to self-monitor. Consider what happened when a good reader made an error in reading the sentence *John went to the store.*

> GOOD READER: John went to the *stone.*
> TEACHER (*after the sentence is completed*): Does that make sense to you?

The student then reread the sentence, correcting his mistake.

Now consider what happened when a struggling reader misread the same sentence.

> STRUGGLING READER: John *want—*
> TEACHER (*interrupting and pointing at the word* went): Look at the vowel in that word.

This interruption led to a bit of unsuccessful word work by the student, followed by the teacher pronouncing the word for him. The student then continued to read.

> STRUGGLING READER: … to the *story.*
> TEACHER: That e is a silent e. Try it again.

How can we be surprised when these different instructional moves create two different types of readers? Unfortunately, my current observations have found that reading instruction is continuing to separate students into two groups—good readers who self-regulate, and struggling readers who stop after almost every word and look up at their teacher for a cue (Allington, 2012). These differences are not inherent in the struggling readers; rather, they're caused by variations in where teachers direct the students' attention. Good readers learn to pay attention to making sense; struggling readers learn to focus on letters and sounds while paying almost no attention to making sense of what they read.

Refining Oral-Reading Practice

To avoid the harm inherent in the overuse and misuse of oral-reading practice, consider the following recommendations:

- Use oral reading selectively. By the middle of 1st grade, most reading should be done silently.
- If you elect to have students read a text aloud, consciously bite your tongue as they read. Wait until the student has completed at least a full sentence before you interrupt, and then interrupt with a comment that encourages the student to self-regulate.
- Ensure that other students who might be following along or listening to the student read aloud also do not interrupt the reader.
- If you're concerned that you cannot monitor the accuracy of students' reading when they read silently, remember that all you really need to do is ask them to retell what they've read. Misreadings become obvious during retellings.

Move 2. Asking Low-Level Questions

The second misguided but common instructional move that I observe in classrooms is asking an interminable number of low-level, literal questions after (or during) reading. I know that the teacher manuals that accompany commercial reading series are filled with such questions. I'm unsure why, when not a single study demonstrates that this practice actually leads to improved reading comprehension.

Too many of the reading lessons I observe focus on these trivial questions while ignoring how well kids actually understand the text they just read. Sadly, except in a few exemplary classrooms, I almost never witness true literate conversations—the kind that people outside classrooms engage in to make meaning of a text they care about, whether a newspaper article, a memo from the school superintendent, a novel, or a biblical passage.

The Need for Literate Conversations

Imagine that you're sitting in a coffee shop one morning reading the local newspaper when a friend walks in and asks, "Have you read the story about the tornado in Johnsonville?" You respond, "Yes, I just finished it." If your friend were then to subject you to the sort of low-level questions found in most reading series ("What was the fire chief's name?" "What color was the car that was destroyed?") you would probably look at her somewhat grumpily and wonder what was wrong with her. Instead, your friend would be more likely to ask something along the lines of, "That tornado was terrible, wasn't it?" You might respond, "Yes, it was a miracle that nobody was killed!" Your friend might respond with a comment about the article's assessment of Johnsonville's emergency alert system. And thus the literate conversation would begin.

The same sort of literate conversation occurs when someone has read the novel you are currently reading. Two literate adults do not quiz each other on low-level, factual details in the texts they've both read. Instead, they often begin with something like, "How do you like that book?" The literate conversation then follows.

It's unfortunate that our classrooms so often replace literate conversations with interrogations about trivial details. Unfortunate, because we have good evidence that engaging students in literate conversations with their peers is a powerful instructional strategy for fostering both short- and long-term reading comprehension (see Fall, Webb, & Chudowsky, 2000; Malloy & Gambrell, 2011; Nystrand, 2006). Classroom discussions do not need to take up vast amounts of instructional time; research has demonstrated that even brief opportunities for discussion can improve students' understanding of texts and their performance on traditional assessments of reading comprehension (Applebee, Langer, Nystrand, & Gamoran, 2003).

In a study of high-poverty schools, Taylor and colleagues (Taylor, Pearson, Clark, & Walpole, 2000; Taylor, Pearson, Peterson, & Rodriguez, 2003) found that more effective teachers asked five times as many higher-order questions and offered twice as many opportunities for discussion as less effective teachers did. The more effective teachers were also more likely to ask students to respond in writing to higher-order questions. Writing after reading, holding classroom conversations about texts that students have read, and responding to higher-order questions are all linked to higher student achievement. But none of these three instructional moves are routinely observed during classroom reading lessons.

Why Do We Stick with the Trivial?

Given the evidence that low-level interrogation routines are ineffective, why do they continue to be such a common instructional move? One reason may be the current practice of labeling the ability to answer multiple-choice questions on standardized achievement tests as "reading comprehension."

A second factor may be the widespread use of commercial core reading programs that provide almost no suggestions for discussion. Twenty years ago, a colleague and I noted that 98 percent of the questions offered in a commercial reading series were low-level, literal questions (Allington & Weber, 1993). More recent research shows that this proportion seems to be holding true in core reading programs (Dewitz, Jones, & Leahy, 2009).

Third, there's evidence that most teachers are ill-prepared to initiate and manage classroom discussions. Kucan, Hapgood, and Palincsar (2011) found that relatively few elementary teachers were skilled in developing high-quality classroom discussions. Only 15 percent of the teachers they observed could specify the difficulties that students might have with the texts they were given. Most of the teachers did not offer effective support; instead of leading discussions flexibly, they relied on probing for general information and directing students to reread.

Improving Classroom Discussions

This research suggests that teachers must begin to develop their expertise in initiating and managing classroom discussions. Because most students have had little experience with discussion, teachers will likely need to develop students' ability to engage one another as conversational partners.

One instructional move that you can use to do this is *turn, pair, and share*—having students turn to a student sitting nearby and talk, even briefly, about a text they have just read or listened to. You might initiate turn, pair, and share by providing a specific structure—for example, requiring that one student talk for the first minute of the activity, followed by a minute for the other student, and ending with a minute in which both students are free to take turns talking to each other.

It may also be useful to model how such conversations might proceed and to help students learn appropriate ways to disagree or challenge a response (for example, by saying "I disagree, and here's why"). For teachers worried about the volume of the noise created when multiple pairs are discussing the text, remember that you can model "whisper talk" as an alternative to full, and often loud, conversation.

A specific turn, pair, and share prompt might be to ask students to discuss whether a character in the story reminds them of anyone. Alternatively, you could ask students to discuss their responses to a higher-order question about the text that they have read. For example, when students are reading *The One and Only Ivan* by Katherine Applegate (HarperCollins, 2012), you might ask, "Do you think that animals really remember things that happened long ago the way Ivan recalled what had happened to his mother and father?" After a few minutes, you can ask one or more pairs to share how their discussion concluded.

Turn, pair, and share enables students to talk through their understandings of what they have been reading. As students develop greater capacity to engage in peer-to-peer discussion, you can ask pairs to jointly write about what they have been discussing. As always, providing a model of what this writing might look like will ease students into this more complex task.

Don't be surprised if many students appear confused or incompetent when you first integrate paired discussions into instruction. Be patient; nothing worthwhile is easy to accomplish. Start with brief turn, pair, and share sessions. Over time, as students become more competent, you can extend sessions and broaden them so the groupings are no longer restricted to pairs but include three to five conversation partners.

Of course, strategies like turn, pair, and share—which enable every student to participate—take more time than teacher-managed discussions in which only a few students are usually involved. But engaging students in literate conversations about what they've been reading must become a common instructional move. You can find time for such discussions by restricting the number of low-level literal questions you ask.

Time to Reconsider

In the end, students are more likely to learn what was taught than to learn what was never taught. Because of schools' overemphasis on oral reading, our students have demonstrated improved oral-reading rates and accuracy but have failed to demonstrate self-regulation or better reading comprehension. Because of schools' failure to make literate conversations a staple of reading instruction, our students daily demonstrate their ability to respond to low-level questions while failing to demonstrate higher-order understanding of what they read. To make literacy instruction more effective, we need to reconsider and fine-tune these common instructional moves.

References

Allington, R. L. (1980). Teacher interruption behaviors during primary grade oral reading. *Journal of Educational Psychology, 72*, 371–377.

Allington, R. L. (1984). Content coverage and contextual reading in reading groups. *Journal of Reading Behavior, 16*(1), 85–96.

Allington, R. L. (2012). *What really matters for struggling readers: Designing research-based programs* (3rd ed.). Boston: Pearson.

Allington, R. L., & Weber, R. M. (1993). Questioning questions in teaching and learning from texts. In B. Britton, A. Woodward, & M. Binkley (Eds.), *Learning from textbooks: Theory and practice* (pp. 47–68). Hillsdale, NJ: Erlbaum.

Applebee, A. N., Langer, J. A., Nystrand, M., & Gamoran, A. (2003). Discussion-based approaches to developing understanding: Classroom instruction and student performance in middle and high school English. *American Educational Research Journal, 40*(3), 685–730.

Dewitz, P., Jones, J., & Leahy, S. (2009). Comprehension strategy instruction in core reading programs. *Reading Research Quarterly, 44*(2), 102–126.

Fall, R., Webb, N. M., & Chudowsky, N. (2000). Group discussion and large-scale language arts assessment: Effects on students' comprehension. *American Educational Research Journal, 37*(4), 911–941.

Gamse, B. C., Jacob, R. T., Horst, M., Boulay, B., & Unlu, F. (2009). *Reading First impact study: Final report* (No. NCEE 2009-4038). Washington, DC: National Center for Education Evaluation and Regional Assistance, Institute of Education Sciences, U.S. Department of Education.

Kucan, L., Hapgood, S., & Palincsar, A. S. (2011). Teachers specialized knowledge for supporting student comprehension in text-based discussions. *Elementary School Journal, 112*(1), 61–82.

Malloy, J. A., & Gambrell, L. B. (2011). The contribution of discussion to reading comprehension and critical thinking. In A. McGill-Franzen & R. L. Allington (Eds.), *The handbook of reading disability research* (pp. 253–261). New York: Routledge.

Mosenthal, P. B. (1977). Psycholinguistic properties of aural and visual comprehension as determined by children's abilities to comprehend syllogisms. *Reading Research Quarterly, 12*, 55–92.

Nystrand, M. (2006). Research on the role of classroom discourse as it affects reading comprehension. *Research in the Teaching of English, 40*, 392–412.

Taylor, B. M., Pearson, P. D., Clark, K., & Walpole, S. (2000). Effective schools and accomplished teachers: Lessons about primary grade reading instruction in low income schools. *Elementary School Journal, 101*, 121–165.

Taylor, B. M., Pearson, P. D., Peterson, D. S., & Rodriguez, M. C. (2003). Reading growth in high-poverty classrooms: The influences of teacher practices that encourage cognitive engagement in literacy learning. *Elementary School Journal, 104*(1), 4–28.

Torgeson, J. K., & Hudson, R. F. (2006). Reading fluency: Critical issues for struggling readers. In S. J. Samuels & A. E. Farstrup (Eds.), *What research has to say about fluency instruction* (pp. 130–158). Newark, DE: International Reading Association.

Richard L. Allington (rallingt@utk.edu) is professor of education at the University of Tennessee and past president of the International Reading Association and the National Reading Conference.

Originally published in the October 2014 issue of *Educational Leadership*, 72(2): pp. 16–21.

Reading Disability and the Brain

Sally E. Shaywitz and Bennett A. Shaywitz

Neurological science and reading research provide the scientific knowledge we need to ensure that almost every child becomes a successful reader.

The past decade has witnessed extraordinary progress in our understanding of the nature of reading and reading difficulties. Never before have rigorous science (including neuroscience) and classroom instruction in reading been so closely linked. For the first time, educators can turn to well-designed, scientific studies to determine the most effective ways to teach reading to beginning readers, including those with reading disability (National Reading Panel, 2000).

What does the evidence tell us? Several lines of investigation have found that reading originates in and relies on the brain systems used for spoken language. In addition, accumulating evidence sheds light on the nature of reading disability, including its definition, prevalence, longitudinal course, and probable causes. Although the work is relatively new, we have already made great progress in identifying the neural systems used for reading, identifying a disruption in these systems in struggling readers, and understanding the neural mechanisms associated with the development of fluent reading.

Reading and Spoken Language

Spoken language is instinctive—built into our genes and hardwired in our brains. Learning to read requires us to take advantage of what nature has provided: a biological module for language.

For the object of the reader's attention (print) to gain entry into the language module, a truly extraordinary transformation must occur. The reader must convert the print on the page into a linguistic code: the phonetic code, the only code recognized and accepted by the language system. Unless the reader-to-be can convert the printed characters on the page into the phonetic code, these letters remain just a bunch of lines and circles, totally devoid of meaning. The written symbols have no inherent meaning of their own but stand, rather, as surrogates for the sounds of speech (Shaywitz, 2003).

To break the code, the first step beginning readers must take involves spoken language. Readers must develop *phonemic awareness*: They must discover that the words they hear come apart into smaller pieces of sound (Shaywitz, 2003).

On the basis of highly reliable scientific evidence, investigators in the field have now reached a strong consensus: Reading reflects language, and reading disability reflects a deficit within the language system. Results from large and well-studied populations with reading disability confirm that in young school-age children (Fletcher et al., 1994; Stanovich & Siegel, 1994) and in adolescents (Shaywitz et al., 1999), a weakness in accessing the sounds of spoken language represents the most robust and specific correlate of reading disability (Morris et al., 1998). Such findings form the foundation for the most successful, evidence-based interventions designed to improve reading (National Reading Panel, 2000).

Understanding Reading Disability

Reading disability, or *developmental dyslexia*, is characterized by an unexpected difficulty in reading in children and adults who otherwise possess the intelligence, motivation, and education necessary for developing accurate and fluent reading (Lyon, 1995; Lyon, Shaywitz, & Shaywitz, 2003). Dyslexia is the most common and most carefully studied of the learning disabilities, affecting 80 percent of all individuals identified as learning disabled and an estimated 5–17 percent of all children and adults in the United States (Shaywitz, 2003).

Incidence and Distribution of Dyslexia

Recent epidemiological data indicate that like hypertension and obesity, reading ability occurs along a continuum. Reading disability falls on the left side of the bell-shaped curve representing the normal distribution of reading ability (Shaywitz, Escobar, Shaywitz, Fletcher, & Makuch, 1992).

Dyslexia runs in families: One-fourth to one-half of all children who have a parent with dyslexia also have the disorder (Scarborough, 1990), and if dyslexia affects one child in the family, it is likely to affect half of his or her siblings. Recent studies have identified a number of genes involved in dyslexia (Fisher & DeFries, 2002).

Good evidence, based on surveys of randomly selected populations of children, now indicates that dyslexia affects boys and girls equally (Flynn & Rahbar, 1994; Shaywitz, Shaywitz, Fletcher, & Escobar, 1990; Wadsworth, DeFries, Stevenson, Gilger, & Pennington, 1992). Apparently, the long-held belief that only boys suffer from dyslexia reflected bias in school-identified samples: The more disruptive behavior of boys results in their being referred for evaluation more often, whereas girls who struggle to read are more likely to sit quietly in their seats and thus be overlooked.

Longitudinal studies (Bruck, 1992; Fletcher, 1996; Francis, Shaywitz, Stuebing, Shaywitz, & Scarborough, 1984; Shaywitz et al., 1995) indicate that dyslexia is a persistent, chronic condition rather than a transient "developmental lag." Children do not outgrow reading difficulties. The evidence-based interventions now available, however, can result in improved reading in virtually all children.

Neurobiological Origins of Dyslexia

For more than a century, physicians and scientists have suspected that dyslexia has neurobiological origins. Until recently, however, they had no way to examine the brain systems that we use while reading. Within the last decade, the dream of scientists, educators, and struggling readers has come true: New advances in technology enable us to view the working brain as it attempts to read.

Perhaps the most convincing evidence for a neurobiological basis of dyslexia comes from the rapidly accumulating and converging data from functional brain imaging investigations. The process of functional brain imaging is quite simple. When we ask an individual to perform a discrete cognitive task, that task places processing demands on specific neural systems in the brain. Through such techniques as functional magnetic resonance imaging (fMRI), we can measure the changes that take place in neural activity in particular brain regions as the brain meets those demands. Because fMRI uses no ionizing radiation and requires no injections, it is noninvasive and safe. We can use it to examine children or adults on multiple occasions.

Using functional brain imaging, scientists around the world have discovered not only the brain basis of reading but also a glitch in the neural circuitry for reading in children and adults who struggle to read. Our studies and those of other investigators have identified three regions involved in reading, all located on the left side of the brain. In the front of the brain, Broca's area (technically the inferior frontal gyrus) is involved in articulation and word analysis. Two areas located in the back of the brain are involved in word analysis (the parieto-temporal region) and in fluent reading (the occipito-temporal region, also referred to as the word form area).

Studies of dyslexic readers document an underactivation of the two systems in the back of the brain together with an overactivation of Broca's area in the front of the brain. The struggling readers appear to be turning to the frontal region, which is responsible for articulating spoken words, to compensate for the fault in the systems in the back of the brain.

Researchers have observed this neurobiological signature of dyslexic readers across cultures and across different languages (Paulesu et al., 2001). The observation of this same pattern in both children and adults supports the view that reading difficulties, including the neural disruption, do not go away with maturity. To prevent failure for students with reading disability, we must identify the disability early and provide effective reading programs to address the students' needs.

The Importance of Fluency

In addition to identifying the neural systems used for reading, research has now revealed which systems the brain uses in two important phases in the acquisition of literacy.

Beginning reading—breaking the code by slowly, analytically sounding out words—calls on areas in the front of the brain (Broca's area) and in the back of the brain (the parieto-temporal region).

But an equally important phase in reading is fluency—rapid, automatic reading that does not require attention or effort. A fluent reader looks at a printed word and instantly knows all the important information about that word. Fluent reading develops as the reader builds brain connections that eventually represent an exact replica of the word—a replica that has integrated the word's pronunciation, spelling, and meaning.

Fluency occurs step-by-step. After systematically learning letters and their sounds, children go on to apply this knowledge to sound out words slowly and analytically. For example, for the word "back," a child may initially represent the word by its initial and final consonants: "b—k." As the child progresses, he begins to fill in the interior vowels, first making some errors—reading "back" as "bock" or "beak," for example—and eventually sounding out the word correctly. Part of the process of becoming a skilled reader is forming successively more detailed and complete representations of familiar words (Shaywitz, 2003).

After the child has read the word "back" correctly over and over again, his brain has built and reinforced an exact model of the word. He now reads that word fluently—accurately, rapidly, and effortlessly. Fluency pulls us into reading. A student who reads fluently reads for pleasure and for information; a student who is not fluent will probably avoid reading.

In a study involving 144 children, we identified the brain region that makes it possible for skilled readers to read automatically (Shaywitz et al., 2002). We found that the more proficiently a child read, the more he or she activated the occipito-temporal region (or word form area) in the back of the brain. Other investigators have observed that this brain region responds to words that are presented rapidly (Price, Moore, & Frackowiak, 1996). Once a word is represented in the word form area, the reader recognizes that word instantly and effortlessly. This word form system appears to predominate when a reader has become fluent. As a result of this finding, we now know that development of the word form area in the left side of the brain is a key component in becoming a skilled, fluent reader.

Helping Struggling Readers Become More Fluent

Our study of 144 children also revealed that struggling readers compensate as they get older, developing alternate reading systems in the front of the brain and in the *right* side of the brain—a functioning system, but, alas, not an automatic one (Shaywitz, 2003). These readers do not develop the critical left-side word form region necessary for rapid, automatic reading. Instead, they call on the alternate secondary pathways. This strategy enables them to read, but much more slowly and with greater effort than their classmates.

This research evidence of a disruption in the normal reading pathways provides a neurobiological target for reading interventions. In a new study (Shaywitz et al., 2003), we hypothesized that an evidence-based, phonologically mediated reading intervention would help dyslexic readers develop the fast-paced word form systems serving skilled reading, thus improving their reading accuracy and fluency. Under the supervision of Syracuse University professor Benita Blachman, we provided 2nd and 3rd grade struggling readers daily with 50 minutes of individual tutoring that was systematic and explicit, focusing on helping the students understand the *alphabetic principle,* or how letters and combinations of letters represent the sounds of speech.

Students received eight months (105 hours) of intervention during the school year in addition to their regular classroom reading instruction. The experimental intervention replaced any additional reading help that the students might have received in school. Certified teachers who had taken part in an intensive training program provided the tutoring.

Immediately after the yearlong intervention, students in the experiment made significant gains in reading fluency and demonstrated increased activation in left hemisphere regions, including the inferior frontal gyrus and the parieto-temporal region. One year after the experimental intervention ended, these students were reading accurately and fluently and were activating all three left-side brain regions used by good readers. A control group of struggling readers receiving school-based, primarily nonphonological reading instruction had not activated these reading systems.

These data demonstrate that an intensive, evidence-based reading intervention brings about significant and durable changes in brain organization so that struggling readers' brain activation patterns come to resemble those of typical readers. If we provide intervention at an early age, then we can improve reading fluency and facilitate the development of the neural systems that underlie skilled reading.

Evidence-Based Effective Reading Instruction

In addition to new neurological research on the nature of reading, educators can draw on a body of rigorous, well-designed, scientific studies to guide reading instruction. In 1998, the U.S. Congress mandated the National Reading Panel to develop rigorous scientific criteria for evaluating reading research, apply these criteria to existing reading research, identify the most effective teaching methods, and then make findings accessible for parents and teachers. As a member of the Panel, I can attest to its diligence. After two years of work, the Panel issued its report (2000).

The major findings of the report indicate that in order to read, all children must be taught alphabetics, comprising phonemic awareness and phonics; reading fluency; vocabulary; and strategies for reading comprehension. These elements must be taught systematically, comprehensively, and explicitly; it is inadequate to present the foundational skills of phonemic awareness and phonics incidentally, casually, or fragmentally. Children do not learn how letters represent sounds by osmosis; we must teach them this skill explicitly. Once a child has mastered these foundational skills, he or she must be taught how to read words fluently.

Good evidence now indicates that we can teach reading fluency by means of repeated oral reading with feedback and guidance. Using these methods (described in detail in Shaywitz, 2003, pp. 176–246), we can teach almost every child to read. It is crucial to align all components of a program with one another—for example, to provide so-called decodable booklets that give the student practice in the specific letter-sound linkages we are teaching. The use of decodable booklets enables the repeated practice necessary to build the automatic systems in the word form region that lead to fluent reading.

Neuroscience and Reading Research Agree

We are now in an era of evidence-based education. Objective scientific evidence—provided by brain imaging studies and by the National Reading Panel's rigorous scientific review of the literature—has replaced reliance on philosophy or opinion.

In considering a reading program, educators should ask several key questions:

- Is there scientific evidence that the program is effective?
- Was the program or its methodology reviewed by the National Reading Panel?
- In reading instruction, are phonemic awareness and phonics taught systematically and explicitly?
- How are students taught to approach an unfamiliar word? Do they feel empowered to try to analyze and sound out an unknown word first rather than guess the word from the pictures or context?
- Does the program also include plenty of opportunities for students to practice reading, develop fluency, build vocabulary, develop reading comprehension strategies, write, and listen to and discuss stories (Shaywitz, 2003)?

Children are only 7 or 8 years old once in their lifetime. We cannot risk teaching students with unproven programs. We now have the scientific knowledge to ensure that almost every child can become a successful reader. Awareness of the new scientific knowledge about reading should encourage educators to insist that reading programs used in their schools reflect what we know about the science of reading and about effective reading instruction.

References

Bruck, M. (1992). Persistence of dyslexics' phonological awareness deficits. *Developmental Psychology*, *28*(5), 874–886.

Fisher, S., & DeFries, J. C. (2002). Developmental dyslexia: Genetic dissection of a complex cognitive trait. *Nature Reviews Neuroscience*, *3*, 767–780.

Fletcher, J., Shaywitz, S., Shankweiler, D., Katz, L., Liberman, I., Stuebing, K., et al. (1994). Cognitive profiles of reading disability: Comparisons of discrepancy and low achievement definitions. *Journal of Educational Psychology*, *86*(1), 6–23.

Flynn, J., & Rahbar, M. (1994). Prevalence of reading failure in boys compared with girls. *Psychology in the Schools*, *31*, 66–71.

Francis, D. J., Shaywitz, S. E., Stuebing, K. K., Shaywitz, B. A., & Fletcher, J. M. (1996). Developmental lag versus deficit models of reading disability: A longitudinal, individual growth curves analysis. *Journal of Educational Psychology, 88*(1), 3–17.

Lyon, G. R. (1995). Toward a definition of dyslexia. *Annals of Dyslexia, 45*, 3–27.

Lyon, G. R., Shaywitz, S. E., & Shaywitz, B. A. (2003). A definition of dyslexia. *Annals of Dyslexia, 53*, 1–14.

Morris, R. D., Stuebing, K. K., Fletcher, J. M., Shaywitz, S. E., Lyon, G. R., Shankweiler, D. P., et al. (1998). Subtypes of reading disability: Variability around a phonological core. *Journal of Educational Psychology, 90*, 347–373.

National Reading Panel. (2000). *Teaching children to read: An evidence-based assessment of the scientific research literature on reading and its implications for reading instruction.* Washington, DC: National Institute of Child Health and Human Development.

Paulesu, E., Demonet, J. F., Fazio, F., McCrory, E., Chanoine, V., Brunswick, N., et al. (2001). Dyslexia-cultural diversity and biological unity. *Science, 291*, 2165–2167.

Price, C., Moore, C., & Frackowiak, R. S. J. (1996). The effect of varying stimulus rate and duration on brain activity during reading. *Neuroimage, 3*(1), 40–52.

Scarborough, H. S. (1984). Continuity between childhood dyslexia and adult reading. *British Journal of Psychology, 75*, 329–348.

Scarborough, H. S. (1990). Very early language deficits in dyslexic children. *Child Development, 61*, 1728–1743.

Shaywitz, B. A., Holford, T. R., Holahan, J. M., Fletcher, J. M., Stuebing, K. K., Francis, D. J., et al. (1995). A Matthew effect for IQ but not for reading: Results from a longitudinal study. *Reading Research Quarterly, 30*(4), 894–906.

Shaywitz, B. A., Shaywitz, S., Blachman, B., Pugh, K., Fullbright, R., Skudlarski, P., et al. (2003). *Development of left occipito-temporal systems for skilled reading following a phonologically-based intervention in children.* Paper presented at the Organization for Human Brain Mapping, New York.

Shaywitz, B. A., Shaywitz, S. E., Pugh, K. R., Mencl, W. E., Fullbright, R. K., Skudlarski, P., et al. (2002). Disruption of posterior brain systems for reading in children with developmental dyslexia. *Biological Psychiatry, 52*, 101–110.

Shaywitz, S. (2003). *Overcoming dyslexia: A new and complete science-based program for reading problems at any level.* New York: Knopf.

Shaywitz, S. E., Escobar, M. D., Shaywitz, B. A., Fletcher, J. M., & Makuch, R. (1992). Evidence that dyslexia may represent the lower tail of a normal distribution of reading ability. *New England Journal of Medicine, 326*(3), 145–150.

Shaywitz, S. E., Fletcher, J. M., Holahan, J. M., Schneider, A. E., Marchione, K. E., Stuebing, K. K., et al. (1999). Persistence of dyslexia: The Connecticut Longitudinal Study at adolescence. *Pediatrics, 104*, 1351–1359.

Shaywitz, S. E., Shaywitz, B. A., Fletcher, J. M., & Escobar, M. D. (1990). Prevalence of reading disability in boys and girls: Results of the Connecticut Longitudinal Study. *Journal of the American Medical Association, 264*(8), 998–1002.

Stanovich, K. E., & Siegel, L. S. (1994). Phenotypic performance profile of children with reading disabilities: A regression-based test of the phonological-core variable-difference model. *Journal of Educational Psychology, 86*(1), 24–53.

Wadsworth, S. J., DeFries, J. C., Stevenson, J., Gilger, J. W., & Pennington, B. F. (1992). Gender ratios among reading-disabled children and their siblings as a function of parental impairment. *Journal of Child Psychology and Psychiatry, 33*(7), 1229–1239.

Sally E. Shaywitz (sally.shaywitz@yale.edu) is Professor of Pediatrics and **Bennett A. Shaywitz** (bennett.shaywitz@yale.edu) is Professor of Pediatrics and Neurology at the Yale University School of Medicine. They are Codirectors of the National Institute of Child Health and Human Development—Yale Center for the Study of Learning and Attention. Sally E. Shaywitz's most recent book is *Overcoming Dyslexia* (Knopf, 2003).

Originally published in the March 2004 issue of *Educational Leadership, 61*(6): pp. 6–11.

Study Guide for *On Developing Readers: Readings from Educational Leadership*

Naomi Thiers

Ideas to try out individually or in a study group.

Helping all students become skilled readers is an unusually complex task. The articles in this collection reflect that complexity, exploring both the practical aspects of teaching reading and the deeper ideas and controversies associated with the field. These questions and activities—which you can try out individually or in a study group—will help you get the most out of selected articles.

What We Must—and *Mustn't*—Do to Build Readers

In his articles in this collection, literacy researcher Richard Allington describes six practices research has consistently shown are part of effective reading instruction ("Every Child, Every Day" by Allington and Rachael Gabriel) and two common ineffective practices we should stop doing ("Reading Moves: What Not to Do").

In addition to practices many teachers probably know work—like giving students a choice of texts and reading aloud to kids—Allington mentions the practice of frequently having students talk with one another about their reading. He and Gabriel assert that "time for students to talk about their reading and writing ... provides measurable benefits in comprehension, motivation, and even language competence." Yet struggling readers are often given less time than stronger readers to talk with peers about texts.

- Does the research presented in Allington and Gabriel's piece about the power of peer dialogue to improve students' reading comprehension surprise you?
- During the next few weeks, take note of how often your students talk with one another in a meaningful way about something they're reading. Examine your curriculum with an eye for how much student talk about texts is embedded. Is peer dialogue lacking in your classroom? How, realistically, might you increase it?

Read what Allington says about the common ineffective practices of having students read aloud and asking students low-level questions on their reading.

- How often do you use these or similar practices in the classroom? On the basis of Allington's suggestions, how might you improve your use of these practices?
- Questions about reading are common in all classrooms, not just reading classrooms. What kinds of questions do you ask students about their reading? Select an upcoming reading assignment and generate a list of questions you might ask students about it. Which questions lead to the kind of literate conversations Allington says are typical among adults?
- Even though research has shown that oral reading and low-level questioning are not effective, these practices continue to

be common. Why do you think teachers stick with practices that don't work?

Toward a Balanced Reading Diet

The Common Core State Standards recommend that K–12 students read more informational text. In his article "You Want Me to Read What?!" Timothy Shanahan says it's crucial to get more nonfiction into schools—nonfiction that goes beyond memoirs and biographies, which rely on narrative structures. Consider the research Shanahan mentions showing that literary texts dominate reading selections in U.S. schools and the reasons he lists why it's important to change this trend.

- Do you agree with Shanahan's argument that kids need to read more informational text? Do you believe proficiency in such reading will facilitate success in college and careers?
- Do a quick tally of the reading materials you make available to students. Roughly, is there an equal amount of literary texts, informational texts on subjects like science, math, and history, and what Shanahan calls "literary nonfiction" (like biographies)? If the amount of informational readings is less than the other categories, list a few ways you might remedy the disparity.

Doing a close reading of an informational text, one that lets the reader gain everything the piece of writing has to offer, is work, asserts Mary Ehrenworth ("Unlocking the Secrets of Complex Text"). This work must generate its own rewards if kids are to pursue such reading wholeheartedly. The texts likely to deliver this payoff, Ehrenworth claims, are "those that kids find inherently fascinating ... real texts that real people read for knowledge and pleasure."

Try this activity to discover which texts will be most enticing for the kids you teach. Ask each of your students to list several specific nonfiction books, magazines, or whatever that they absolutely love to read. Make sure each kid names something, and cast the net wide, from young adult novels to manga.

- Share your lists in your study group. What kinds of texts are student favorites? What surprises you about their choices?
- Do you have any of these specific texts—or others like them—in your school and classroom library? If so, how might you get them into more students' hands? If not, can you add some of them?
- Ehrenworth says texts that reward the work of close reading must be "accessible, engaging, and complex." The texts your students love are likely accessible and engaging. Sample a few of their recommendations to see which ones are also *complex*. Have each group member describe one piece of reading students love that is truly complex—and discuss how the author makes this text complex *and* engaging.

Creating Readers for Life

Several authors in this collection discuss practices that encourage or discourage a love of reading in students. Kelly Gallagher ("Reversing Readicide") explains how teachers often either overteach works of literature by requiring students to analyze every page, or underteach great works by not giving the students the background knowledge and support they need to understand what they're reading. In "Becoming a Classroom of Readers," Donalyn Miller suggests that free choice and an end to teaching whole-class novels are the keys to helping students become life-long readers.

- If you are an English or reading teacher, how do you approach teaching literature? Compare your strategies to Gallagher's descriptions of overteaching and underteaching. Do you see yourself following either of these patterns? What effect do you

believe it is having on your students, and how might you adjust your strategies?
- How much time do you give students to read in class? How could you find more time for in-class reading? Miller suggests eliminating warm-up and "when you are done" activities. Would this work for your students?
- Do you teach whole-class novels? What do you see as the benefits and drawbacks of this approach? How might you improve your whole-class novel units? Or would you consider following Miller's advice and eliminate them entirely?
- How much choice do you give your students in their reading? How do you respond when they are reading something that, in your view, lacks merit or is insufficiently challenging?

Naomi Thiers is an Associate Editor for *Educational Leadership*.

EL Takeaways
On Developing Readers

"The notion that children must learn to read before they can read to learn is a relic of the past." —*Nell K. Duke*

"Research has demonstrated that access to self-selected texts improves students' reading performance, but no evidence indicates that workbooks, photocopies, or computer tutorial programs have ever done so." —*Richard L. Allington*

"Too many readers who possess the reading skills needed for academic tasks see reading as a school job—not an activity in which they would willingly engage outside school." —*Donalyn Miller*

"Literature study offers students windows to other worlds, other cultures, other times. It poses intellectual challenges, demanding that students stretch and grow." —*Carol Jago*

"Just as it's impossible to build muscle without weight or resistance, it's impossible to build robust reading skills without reading challenging texts." —*Timothy Shanahan, Douglas Fisher, and Nancy Frey*

"We need to share with students the purpose for reading a given text—such as to find a specific piece of information or to read the text and form an opinion." —*Cris Tovani*

Related ASCD Resources

At the time of publication, the following ASCD resources were available (ASCD stock numbers appear in parentheses). For up-to-date information about ASCD resources, go to www.ascd.org. You can search the complete archives of *Educational Leadership* at http://www.ascd.org/el.

ASCD EDge®
Exchange ideas and connect with other educators interested in math on the social networking site ASCD EDge at http://ascdedge.ascd.org.

Print Products
A Close Look at Close Reading: Teaching Students to Analyze Complex Texts, Grades K–5 by Diane Lapp, Barbara Moss, Maria Grant, and Kelly Johnson (#114008)
A Close Look at Close Reading: Teaching Students to Analyze Complex Texts, Grades 6–12 by Barbara Moss, Diane Lapp, Maria Grant, and Kelly Johnson (#115002)
Building Student Literacy Through Sustained Silent Reading by Steve Gardiner (#105027)
Complex Text Decoded: How to Design Lessons and Use Strategies That Target Authentic Texts by Kathy T. Glass (#115006)
Content-Area Conversations: How to Plan Discussion-Based Lessons for Diverse Language Learners by Douglas Fisher, Nancy Frey, and Carol Rothenberg (#108035)
Reading for Meaning: How to Build Students' Comprehension, Reasoning, and Problem-Solving Skills (A Strategic Teacher PLC Guide) by Harvey F. Silver, Susan C. Morris, and Victor Klein (#110128)
Teaching Reading in the Content Areas: If Not Me, Then Who? 3rd edition by Vicki Urquhart and Dana Frazee (#112024)

PD Online® Courses
Common Core and Literacy Strategies: English Language Arts, 2nd Edition (#PD14OC006M)

For more information: send e-mail to member@ascd.org; call 1-800-933-2723 or 703-578-9600, press 2; send a fax to 703-575-5400; or write to Information Services, ASCD, 1703 N. Beauregard St., Alexandria, VA 22311-1714 USA.

THE WHOLE CHILD

ASCD's Whole Child approach is an effort to transition from a focus on narrowly defined academic achievement to one that promotes the long-term development and success of all children. Through this approach, ASCD supports educators, families, community members, and policymakers as they move from a vision about educating the whole child to sustainable, collaborative actions.

On Developing Readers: Readings from Educational Leadership relates to the **engaged** and **challenged** tenets.

WHOLE CHILD TENETS

1. HEALTHY
Each student enters school healthy and learns about and practices a healthy lifestyle.

2. SAFE
Each student learns in an environment that is physically and emotionally safe for students and adults.

3. ENGAGED
Each student is actively engaged in learning and is connected to the school and broader community.

4. SUPPORTED
Each student has access to personalized learning and is supported by qualified, caring adults.

5. CHALLENGED
Each student is challenged academically and prepared for success in college or further study and for employment and participation in a global environment.

For more about the Whole Child approach, visit **www.wholechildeducation.org**.

LEARN. TEACH. LEAD.

DON'T MISS A SINGLE ISSUE OF ASCD'S AWARD-WINNING MAGAZINE,

 EDUCATIONAL LEADERSHIP

If you belong to a Professional Learning Community, you may be looking for a way to get your fellow educators' minds around a complex topic. Why not delve into a relevant theme issue of *Educational Leadership*, the journal written by educators for educators.

Subscribe now, or buy back issues of ASCD's flagship publication at **www.ascd.org/ELbackissues**.

Single issues cost $7 (for issues dated September 2006–May 2013) or $8.95 (for issues dated September 2013 and later). Buy 10 or more of the same issue, and you'll save 10 percent. Buy 50 or more of the same issue, and you'll save 15 percent. For discounts on purchases of 200 or more copies, contact **programteam@ascd.org**; 1-800-933-2723, ext. 5773.

To see more details about these and other popular issues of *Educational Leadership*, visit **www.ascd.org/ELarchive**.

LEARN. TEACH. LEAD.

1703 North Beauregard Street
Alexandria, VA 22311-1714 USA

www.ascd.org/el

www.ingramcontent.com/pod-product-compliance
Lightning Source LLC
Chambersburg PA
CBHW070617300426
44113CB00010B/1558